PUBLISHED by PARABLES
Earthly Stories with a Heavenly Meaning

SERVANTS OF THE MOST HIGH GOD--BRING MY CHILDREN HOME

A novel by

Rick Stem

Servants Of The Most High God- Bring My Children Home
By Rick Stem

Published By Parables
June, 2021

All Rights Reserved. No part of this book may be reproduced or utilized in any form or by any means, electronic or mechanical, including photocopying, **recording, or by any information storage and retrieval system, without permission in writing from the author. Unless otherwise noted, all Bible verses are drawn from the NIV translation of the Bible.**

Printed in the United States of America

Readers should be aware that Internet Web sites offered as citations and/or sources for further information may have been changed or disappeared between the time this was written and the time it is read.

SERVANTS OF THE MOST HIGH GOD--BRING MY CHILDREN HOME

A novel by

Rick Stem

DEDICATION

I dedicate this book to my five grandchildren: Abraham, Miriam, Penelope, Josiah, and Olive.
May God bless them with the ever-increasing knowledge of His Son, Jesus Christ.

ABOUT THE AUTHOR

Rick was born and raised in Centre County, Pennsylvania. He grew up on the dairy and beef farms his father worked. As a young man, he accepted Jesus Christ as his Lord and Savior and accepted God's calling into the ministry.

Rick graduated from Valley Forge Christian College with a bachelor's degree in Bible. He has served in full-time ministry as a pastor and a pastor of evangelism. He also served in full-time law enforcement as a deputy sheriff and as a police officer. While working in law enforcement, Rick served as a police k-9 handler and trained other police k-9 dog/handler teams as well.

Rick has trained dogs professionally for dog owners for over forty years. Because of his experience in the above, Rick published his first book in 2006 entitled *Seeing God Through The Eyes Of A Dog Trainer*. In 2015 Rick published his second book entitled *The Intercessor*. Rick is a licensed minister with the South Carolina District of the Assemblies of God.

INTRODUCTION

Every day many thousands of people die in many ways and these people never knew it was their last day of life. Most people probably never think about it or the place where they might spend eternity. This book is written to bring about an awareness of death that awaits all people as well as the awareness of a choice of two places to spend eternity--and you the reader will make that choice. This book is written to describe the choice made by those who recognize they are a sinner in need of God's salvation which God provides through His Son, Jesus Christ. The stories in this book describe the choice for heaven for those who put saving faith in Jesus Christ.

This is a story of two of God's holy angels whose service to God is to carry the spirits of Christian believers, when they die, to heaven as Jesus described in Luke 16:22 when Jesus spoke of the angels carrying the beggar, Lazarus's spirit to Abraham's side after he died. The angels and the other characters are fictional characters and the stories they participate in are fictional as well.

The angels discuss realities between themselves and the spirits of the deceased Christian believers before they carry them to heaven so various realities can be shared with the reader. The book is written with eight substories that are written with biblical quotes so as to teach the realities of various subjects--such as what takes place the moment the Christian believer dies, how the spirits of Christian believers get to heaven, a description of what heaven is like as well as the scriptural assurance of the Christian believer meeting Jesus in heaven.

The way to salvation is explained and the assurance of going to heaven when the Christian believer dies is explained as well as the Christian believer's assurance of having eternal life in Jesus Christ. Hopefully, all who read this book will be encouraged, ministered unto, and blessed. But most of all the book is written to exalt the Lord Jesus Christ who died on Calvary's Cross for the sins of the entire world, including you, the reader. It is my prayer that for the reader who has yet to come to Jesus Christ in saving faith will do so. After that, may I encourage you to find a good Bible teaching church where the Holy Spirit can move through its members to minister to you and help you grow in your newfound faith in Jesus Christ. As the Apostle Paul states in Romans 10:11, "As the scripture says, 'Anyone who trusts in Him will never be put to shame.'"

Contents

CHAPTER ONE 1
   Carlos 1
CHAPTER TWO 6
CHAPTER THREE 12
CHAPTER FOUR 16
   Hassan 16
CHAPTER FIVE 20
CHAPTER SIX 26
CHAPTER SEVEN 30
   Marshal 30
CHAPTER EIGHT 33
CHAPTER NINE 39
CHAPTER TEN 44
   Jonathan 44
CHAPTER ELEVEN 47
CHAPTER TWELVE 50
CHAPTER THIRTEEN 54
   Tim 54
CHAPTER FOURTEEN 57
CHAPTER FIFTEEN 62
CHAPTER SIXTEEN 65
   Unnamed 65
CHAPTER SEVENTEEN 68
CHAPTER EIGHTEEN 72
CHAPTER NINETEEN 76
   Sarah 76
CHAPTER TWENTY 80
CHAPTER TWENTY-ONE 84
CHAPTER TWENTY-TWO 88
   Tribulation Saints 88
CHAPTER TWENTY-THREE 92
CHAPTER TWENTY-FOUR 96
CHAPTER TWENTY-FIVE 100

Rick Stem

CHAPTER ONE

Carlos

In the realm of man time is a standard of measure. Most people might think of a second as being the smallest measure of time with which they are familiar. From one second, we learn that sixty seconds equals one minute of time. Sixty minutes of time equals one hour of time. These measurements of time are usually taught and learned in the earliest years of grade school.

In the progression of time, one learns that twenty-four hours equals one day, and that seven days equals one week. Depending on one's calendar system we learn that so many weeks equals one month, and twelve months equals one year. And as we grow older, we find that the measure of time in years takes on an important relevancy--one that yields to the relevancy of how long a life we may live before it all ends in death.

Servants of the Most High God

The scriptures declare that God is eternal and therefore not bound by the same measure of time that man is, though God is very much involved with man during man's lifetime. Psalm 48:14 states, "For such is God, our God forever and ever, He will guide until death." (NASB) Though God is not bound by man's standard of time, yet the Scriptures declare that the eternal God created time. Genesis 1:1-5 states, "In the beginning God created the heavens and the earth. Now the earth was formless and empty, darkness was over the surface of the deep, and the Spirit of God was hovering over the waters. And God said, 'Let there be light,' and there was light. God saw that the light was good, and He separated the light from the darkness. God called the light 'day,' and the darkness He called 'night.' And there was evening, and there was morning--the first day."

Benjamin and Amnon are two of God's holy angels, who are in route to a street in Albuquerque, New Mexico. Benjamin and Amnon serve the Most High God in that they carry the spirits of deceased Christian believers to heaven when they die.

"You know, Amnon, I consider it a privilege to serve God in this capacity," said Benjamin.

"It is definitely an important service," replied Amnon.

"Jesus considered it important enough to make mention of it," replied Benjamin. "Listen to Jesus' words in Luke 16:22 'The time came when the beggar died and the angels carried him to Abraham's side,'" said Benjamin as he quoted Jesus. "From this passage of scripture Christian believers can learn how their spirits get to Heaven when they die," continued Benjamin.

"It is not hard to serve God in faithfulness and obedience," said Amnon, "for the scriptures declare in

Rick Stem

Psalm 148:1-6 'Praise the Lord. Praise the Lord from the heavens, praise Him in the heights above. Praise Him, all his angels, praise Him, all His heavenly hosts. Praise Him sun and moon, praise Him, all you shining stars. Praise Him, you highest heavens and you waters above the skies. Let them praise the name of the Lord, for He commanded, and they were created.'"

"Do not forget when God told his faithful servant, Job, that we angels watched as all of creation was spoken into existence and how we angels gave much praise to God," said Benjamin.

"I remember God telling Job just like it was yesterday," said Amnon as he recited the very words of Job 38:4-7, "Where were you when I laid the earth's foundation? Tell me if you understand. Who marked off its dimensions? Surely you know! Who stretched a measuring line across it? On what were its footings set, or who laid its cornerstone--while the morning stars sang together, and all the angels shouted for joy?"

"I get excited just hearing those words!" said Benjamin. "Who wouldn't get excited watching all of creation come into existence," Benjamin continued.

Amnon with the excitement of a holy angel who loves the service he does for God quoted the very words of Hebrews 1:14, "Are not all angels ministering spirits sent to serve those who will inherit salvation?"

"I too enjoy the ministry we provide for God's spiritual children," replied Benjamin. "Though as angels we never die, yet we who serve God as we do, observe death in the lives of men all the time," said Benjamin.

"But since we deal with the deaths of Christian believers it's really not a sad situation," replied Amnon. Amnon went on to quote the very words of Jesus when he quoted John 3:16-17 "For God so loved the world that He gave his one and only Son, that whoever believes in Him shall not perish but have eternal life. For God did not send His Son into the world to condemn the world, but to save the world through Him."

"Another passage of scripture I like of Jesus providing eternal life is John 11:25-26," said Benjamin. Benjamin went on to quote the words Jesus spoke to His friend, Martha, the sister of Lazarus, a close and dear friend of Jesus who had died, but whom Jesus brought back to life. John 11:25-26 "Jesus said to her, 'I am the resurrection and the life. He who believes in me will live, even though he dies; and whoever lives and believes in me will never die. Do you believe this?'"

"We are continually observing the joy of deceased Christian believers as we carry their spirits to heaven where they for the first time, see the One whom they've committed their saving faith to--Jesus," said Amnon. "It is such an exciting moment to watch as they enter heaven's doorway and there He is, Jesus, to welcome them to their eternal heavenly home," said Amnon.

"It never gets old," replied Benjamin. "I think it's why the Apostle Paul stated in Philippians 1:23 'I am torn between the two: I desire to depart and be with Christ, which is better by far;'" Benjamin continued.

Benjamin and Amnon arrive at their destination-- always early and never late. Since God knows all things, He knows the exact time of death for every human being. Since man does not know the time of their own death, many are surprised and spiritually unprepared to enter eternity. Sadly, many will die in their sins.

Benjamin and Amnon arrive in time for Carlos, a young Christian man who is married to a beautiful Christian wife. Carlos is also the father of two young children who have expressed saving faith in Jesus Christ as taught and exemplified by Carlos and his wife. Carlos is a police officer with the Albuquerque Police Department. Though Carlos has by faith received the salvation of Jesus Christ and received the promise of eternal life, he, like most other people when they die, is totally unaware that today is his last day of life.

Carlos's death will come as a total surprise to him as well as to those who know him and love him. But his death will not be a surprise to God, his heavenly Father, nor to Benjamin and Amnon who have arrived to take him to his heavenly home. In reality, the best lies just ahead for Carlos.

CHAPTER TWO

It was a hot summer night, and Carlos was working the Friday evening shift. It was approximately 8:15 PM when Carlos pulled up to a residence of a domestic violence call. As Carlos arrived on the scene, he observed screams coming from a female subject on the scene and loud threatening language from a male subject on the scene. Carlos knew it was best to wait for backup to arrive before intervening in the situation, but things seemed to be getting out of hand, so he exited his police vehicle while informing dispatch. The other police officer was just a minute away. Carlos approached the male and female subjects while ordering them to separate and be quiet. In response the male subject turned towards Carlos, pulled a handgun out of his pants and aimed the gun at Carlos. Time seemed to stand still as Carlos looked down the barrel of a handgun pointed at him. With a highly elevated sense of survival, Carlos's mind briefly wandered "where is my backup?" As Carlos reached for his holster to pull out his own handgun in defense, the male subject pulled the trigger and in less than a second of time, the bullet struck Carlos, killing him instantly. Backup then arrived on the scene and brought the situation under control.

At the moment of death Carlos's spirit left his body and was immediately delivered into the hands of Benjamin and Amnon just like a newborn baby exits the mother's womb and is delivered into the hands of the doctor at the time of birth. Benjamin and Amnon had been on the scene and waiting for this moment.

"Welcome Carlos," said Benjamin. "Let me introduce ourselves to you. I am Benjamin and this is Amnon. We are two of God's holy angels and we are here to carry your spirit to heaven," Benjamin continued.

"Where exactly is heaven?" Carlos asked.

"The best way for me to describe where heaven is, is for me to quote the words of the Apostle Paul as he describes heaven's location," said Benjamin. Benjamin then quoted 2nd Corinthians 12:2-4 "I know a man in Christ who fourteen years ago was caught up to the third heaven. Whether it was in the body or out of the body I do not know--God knows. And I know that this man--whether in the body or apart from the body I do not know, but God knows--was caught up to Paradise. He heard inexpressible things, things that no one is permitted to tell."

"Don't worry Carlos, we know our way there." said Amnon.

"Am I really dead?" asked Carlos.

"Yes, you really are," replied Amnon.

"I can hardly believe that my life is over," lamented Carlos. "My life seems to have been way too short," continued Carlos.

"You're not the only one who thinks this way Carlos," said Amnon. "In Psalm 144:4, listen to the words of the Psalmist." continued Amnon. "Man is like a breath; his days are like a fleeting shadow." said Amnon.

Servants of the Most High God

"The Psalmist says in Psalm 103:15-16 'As for man, his days are like grass, he flourishes like a flower of the field; the wind blows over it and it is gone, and its place remembers it no more,'" said Benjamin.

"My grandfather died a few years back," said Carlos. "Will I see him in heaven when I get there?" asked Carlos.

Benjamin and Amnon got the biggest smile on their angelic faces. "Carlos, you might not believe this, but Benjamin and I carried your grandfather's spirit to heaven on the day he died," said Amnon.

Carlos then got a big smile on his face (for a spirit) knowing that he would be reunited with his grandfather in heaven. Carlos's grandfather was also his church pastor as he was growing up and Carlos greatly loved and respected his grandfather.

"I've always wondered if we would know other people in heaven," said Carlos.

"The Apostle Paul knew the answer to your question Carlos, and he informed the Thessalonian believers of that answer," said Benjamin. "Listen to what the Apostle Paul told the Thessalonian believers in 1st Thessalonians 4:13-18 as he attempts to comfort those living believers whose loved ones had died and they wondered if they would see their loved ones again in the rapture," Benjamin continued.

Benjamin quoted the Apostle Paul saying, "Brothers, we do not want you to be ignorant about those who fall asleep, or to grieve like the rest of men, who have no hope. We believe that Jesus died and rose again, and so we believe that God will bring with Jesus those who have fallen asleep in Him. According to the Lord's own word, we tell you that we who are still alive, who are left till the coming of the Lord, will certainly not precede those who have fallen asleep. For the Lord himself will come down from heaven, with a loud command, with the voice of the archangel and with the trumpet call of God, and the dead in Christ will rise first. After that we who are still alive and are left will be caught up together with them in the clouds to meet the Lord in the air. And so, we will be with the Lord forever. Therefore, encourage one another with these words."

"Oh no! I forgot about my wife!" exclaimed Carlos. "What about the pain and grief she's going to experience once she learns I've been killed?" Carlos asked with a concerned voice.

"Carlos, no need for you to be concerned--you are dead," said Amnon. "There's nothing you can say, there's nothing you can do," Amnon continued.

"Carlos, your wife is in good hands--she is in God's hands," said Benjamin. "Do you remember the words Jesus spoke to His disciples in John 14:15-18?"

"If you love me, you will obey what I command. And I will ask the Father, and He will give you another Counselor to be with you forever--the Spirit of truth. The world cannot accept Him because it neither sees Him nor knows Him. But you know Him, for He lives with you and will be in you. I will not leave you as orphans; I will come to you."

"Also, Carlos, Romans 8:26-27 reads, 'In the same way, the Spirit helps us in our weakness. We do not know what we ought to pray for, but the Spirit Himself intercedes for us with groans that words cannot express. And He who searches our hearts knows the mind of the Spirit, because the Spirit intercedes for the saints in accordance with God's will,'" said Amnon.

Servants of the Most High God

"Amnon and I do this service all the time," said Benjamin. "The Holy Spirit will get your Christian wife through this painful and grieving time," Benjamin continued.

"Besides, Carlos, heaven is not like the sufferings of this world," said Amnon. "Let me quote Revelation 21:4 which reads, 'He will wipe every tear from their eyes. There will be no more death or mourning or crying or pain, for the old order of things has passed away.'" said Benjamin.

"Carlos, are you ready to go?" asked Amnon. "If so, just relax and we will have you there in just a moment," continued Amnon.

Benjamin and Amnon knew that Carlos was about to experience His greatest joy ever when he steps into heaven and is in awe of the glory of God that radiates in the total environment of heaven. Carlos will truly be living the eternal life Jesus promises those who receive His great salvation. In a moment he will be welcomed into his heavenly home by his Lord and Savior, Jesus Christ. Carlos will also see his grandfather who preceded him in death as well as other loved ones and friends who previously died. And Carlos shall dwell forever in the presence of Jesus.

Carlos's wife will suffer the initial loss of her husband but the Holy Spirit abiding in her life will see her through the grieving and healing process. She knows also according to 1st Thessalonians 4:13-18 that at the resurrection and rapture of the Church she will see Carlos again. Carlos and his wife each will experience the benefits of knowing Jesus Christ personally. Carlos will experience his heavenly home where the sufferings of this earthly life are behind him, and Carlos's wife will experience the benefits of having a personal relationship with Jesus Christ as she continues living this early life. Sadly, the unbelieving world will not share in their experiences.

CHAPTER THREE

It took only a moment of time for Benjamin and Amnon to travel from the first heaven (earth's atmosphere) through the second heaven (outer space) to reach heaven, located in the third heaven where God the Father dwells, according to the Apostle Paul. In John 14:2 Jesus refers to heaven as His Father's house.

"That was quick!" exclaimed Carlos.
"We told you it would only take a moment," replied Benjamin.
"Just straight ahead of you there is an open door leading into heaven," said Amnon.
"Is this door always open?" asked Carlos.
"It's always open," replied Benjamin. "It has to be," continued Benjamin, "because angels are carrying the spirits of deceased Christian believers here to their heavenly home around the clock, 24/7, as you would say in earthly language, Carlos."
"Every day many thousands of people around the world die, not knowing it was their last day of life," said Amnon. "We angels stay busy at carrying the spirits of

deceased Christian believers, or as God would refer to them as His children, to heaven," continued Amnon.

"And even though we stay busy in this wonderful service to God, yet many thousands of people die and instead of going to heaven because of not having put saving faith in Jesus Christ, their spirits go to hell because they failed to believe and accept the salvation of God provided through His Son, Jesus Christ," said Benjamin.

"Let us escort you inside," said Amnon.

Benjamin and Amnon escorted Carlos through the open doorway leading into heaven. Carlos was completely in awe of what he initially was seeing and hearing. With the presence of God, the Father, and the glorified Son of God (Jesus), heaven was a most glorious environment, nothing like Carlos has ever experienced. Heaven is a huge place, filled with the sounds of continuous worship of God the Father and Jesus the Son.

Right off the bat Jesus was standing before Carlos with arms open wide to welcome him to heaven, his eternal heavenly home. With a smile on His face Jesus embraced Carlos and said, "Welcome home, Carlos, I've been praying for you." It was then that Carlos saw the nail prints in Jesus' hands, reminding Carlos that Jesus died on Calvary's Cross for his sins as well as the sins of the whole world.

"It's good to be here," replied Carlos to Jesus. "I would never be here without you dying for my sins and rising from the dead," continued Carlos.

The worship being conducted in heaven did not stop with the arrival of Carlos, but the worship actually included welcoming him to heaven so that everyone in heaven knew he had arrived and was "now home." Meeting Jesus face to face was not only a reward of the saving faith Carlos had put in Jesus, but he experienced something very different and quite unique. As Carlos locked eyes with Jesus, he was experiencing what the Apostle Paul stated in 1st Corinthians 13:12 "Now we see but a poor reflection as in a mirror: then we shall see face to face. Now I know in part; then I shall know fully, even as I am fully known." In fact, everyone Carlos was meeting in heaven he was knowing them though he never met them before. Carlos was experiencing no strangers in heaven but instead was experiencing joyful brotherly fellowship with one another.

"Hey Carlos," said Benjamin as he and Amnon turned Carlos around.
"Look who's here," said Amnon, expressing much happiness to him.
Carlos turned around and there was his grandfather.
"Carlos, it's good to see you!" said Carlos's grandfather.
"It's good to see you too, Pepe`!" exclaimed Carlos.

Pepe` was what Carlos called his grandfather. Carlos and his grandfather embraced each other with a "heavenly" hug exemplifying one of the great blessings of his relationship with God the Father and Jesus His Lord and Savior. Carlos and his grandfather will spend all eternity with Jesus, their Lord, as well as with one another and all the other Christian brothers and sisters who enter heaven.

Rick Stem

"Carlos, heaven is just as great as the scriptures declare," said Carlos's grandfather. "But experiencing it is just too astounding to really describe with words," Carlos's grandfather continued. "But we'll enjoy it together as we wait for the rest of the family to get here," said Carlos's grandfather.

"Enjoy!" exclaimed Benjamin and Amnon to Carlos and his grandfather. "We've got another of God's children to bring home!" shouted Benjamin and Amnon as they sped out the always open door to heaven with the excitement of meeting their next assignment.

CHAPTER FOUR

Hassan

As Benjamin and Amnon sped to their next assignment they reflected on the opportunities to enter into worship every time they carried one of "God's children" home to heaven. Ever since God created the angels, they have always worshipped God because He is worthy of worship.

"Do you remember that day when Jesus invited the Apostle John to visit heaven?" Benjamin asked Amnon. "I remember," replied Benjamin. "He was astounded at the sheer number of angels that he saw worshiping God," Benjamin continued.

"Listen to the words of the Apostle John as recorded in Revelation 5:11-12 of the angelic hosts worshiping God," said Benjamin. "Then I looked and heard the voice of many angels, numbering thousands upon thousands, and ten thousand times ten thousand. They encircled the throne and the living creatures and the elders.

Rick Stem

In a loud voice they sang: 'Worthy is the Lamb, who was slain, to receive power and wealth and wisdom and strength and honor and glory and praise!'"

"It is one thing to observe the angels worshipping God, it is very different to experience it," replied Amnon.

"Ah, worship is so wonderful in heaven with the countless multitudes of God's holy angels and the countless multitudes of God's children worshiping Father and Son!" exclaimed Benjamin.

"How can it not be?" asked Amnon. "When you have God the Father seated on His throne, sovereignly ruling the universe, and Jesus the Son seated on His throne next to the Father making intercession for God's children and then you have God's Holy Spirit before the throne of God. "One can only worship with much adoration because of their being in the very presence of God," continued Amnon.

"I get "goosebumps" of excitement just thinking about it," replied Benjamin.

"Hey Benjamin, do you remember how great worship in heaven was when Lucifer was the worship leader?" asked Amnon.

"Worship in heaven was truly great!" exclaimed Benjamin. "Worship in heaven was great because Lucifer was created in greatness by God," continued Benjamin. Benjamin went on to describe the greatness of Lucifer by quoting God's own words in Ezekiel 28:12-15. "Son of man, take up a lament concerning the king of Tyre and say to him: "This is what the sovereign Lord says: 'You were the model of perfection, full of wisdom and perfect in beauty. You were in Eden, the garden of God; every precious stone adorned you: ruby, topaz and emerald, chrysolite, onyx and jasper, sapphire, turquoise and beryl. Your settings and mountings were made of gold; on the day you were created they were prepared. You were anointed as a guardian cherub, for so I ordained you. You were on the holy mount of God; you walked among the fiery stones. You were blameless in all your ways from the day you were created till wickedness was found in you."

"All of the beautiful stones that adorned Lucifer reflected the magnificence of God's glory so that it appeared that Lucifer was a beautiful angel of light in himself which contributed to his pride," said Amnon.

Amnon went on to speak of Lucifer's fall by quoting the words of God in Isaiah 14:12-14. "How you have fallen from heaven, O morning star, son of the dawn! You have been cast down to the earth, you who once laid low the nations! You said in your heart, I will ascend to heaven; I will raise my throne above the stars of God; I will sit enthroned on the mount of assembly, on the utmost heights of the sacred mountain. I will ascend above the tops of the clouds; I will make myself like the Most High."

"We then watched God demote Lucifer and cast him to the newly created earth for his domain," said Benjamin.

"Lucifer is now called Satan, because he is an adversary to God's children," replied Amnon. "As a matter of fact, Benjamin, listen how the Apostle Paul describes Satan in 2nd Corinthians 4:4," continued Amnon. "The god of this age has blinded the minds of unbelievers, so that they cannot see the light of the gospel of the glory of Christ, who is the image of God."

Benjamin replied back to Amnon by quoting Jesus' description of Satan in John 8:44, "You belong to your father, the devil, and you want to carry out your father's desire. He was a murderer from the beginning, not holding to the truth, for there is no truth in him. When he lies, he speaks his native language, for he is a liar and the father of lies."

"Satan will do whatever he can to keep people from receiving the gospel message of salvation," said Amnon. "Satan will teach people a false teaching and even threaten the lives of those who fail to recant their faith in Jesus Christ," Amnon lamented.

"In light of our service to God I cannot help but be in awe when I see Christian believers hold fast to their saving faith in our creator, Jesus Christ, even to the point of dying for their faith in Jesus," said Benjamin.

"Well then, be prepared for another time of being in such awe as we approach our next assignment," said Amnon.

CHAPTER FIVE

Benjamin and Amnon arrive at a barn in the outskirts of a remote village in Afghanistan. Under the guise of families coming together for eggs, milk and cheese, a few families have come together on this Sunday morning to conduct a Christian church service where believers fellowship with one another, worship the One true God--the God of Israel, and His Son, Jesus Christ through song and music, preaching, and praying for one another's needs.

The Pastor's name is Hassan. Hassan is a former Afghan radicle Islamist who used to not only hunt down Christian believers but also threatened their lives with death if they failed to recant their faith in Jesus Christ as their Lord and Savior. Pastor Hassan has a resume of killing men, women and children who stood firm in their faith in Jesus Christ.

Having grown up in Afghanistan where the country's religion is Islam, Hassan grew up putting faith in the teachings of a false God--Allah, as well as encouraging the killing of those who do not believe in Allah. Hassan was taught that conversion to Christianity was punishable by death. But Christian believers wanting to have a relationship with the true God, voluntarily put their faith in

Jesus who declared in John 14:6 "I am the way and the truth and the life. No one comes to the Father except through me."

Hassan had been pastoring this group of believers for about a year and a half. He had been successful during this time of conducting church ministry without being detected by the radical Islamists who hunt such people down. But Hassan, like those in his congregation, knew it would only be a matter of time before they would be found though no one looked forward to that day, especially Hassan.

Benjamin and Amnon, as well as several other angels were invisibly present in Hassan's church service that morning. Because God had assigned them to this location, they knew today was the day of "going home" for each of the members of this congregation. Benjamin and Amnon, as well as the other angels present observed the worship the members of this congregation gave to God. Under the leading of God's Holy Spirit, the result of singing and giving praise exalted the name of Jesus. As Jesus is glorified in worship one can be reminded of Jesus' own words in Revelation 2:1 "To the angel of the church in Ephesus write: These are the words of Him who holds the seven stars in His right hand and walks among the seven golden lampstands."

As Hassan and his congregation were worshipping God, a loud crash was heard as six radical Islamist soldiers crashed through the barn door and stood there yelling threats to the congregation with semi-automatic weapons pointed at them--all for the result of creating an immediate state of fear. It worked. Especially the women and children who began screaming and crying because they fearfully knew what this could mean. Hassan, the shepherd of his spiritual flock, quickly intervened for his congregation by telling them that things would be alright,

Servants of the Most High God

and that Jesus was in their midst. The members of the radical Islamists group recognized Hassan as being a former member of their group.

"Hey guys, look who it is that we found among this group of Christians!" shouted one of the Islamists.

"Yeah, it's our good buddy Hassan," replied another Islamist sarcastically. "We thought you were dead," the Islamist continued.

"Well, I did die," replied Hassan. "But not that you would understand," continued Hassan.

Hassan was thinking how he might be able to talk his and his congregation's way out of this fearful and dreadful situation. He thought that he might share the Apostle Paul's conversion experience as a parallel to his own conversion in hopes that his "good buddies" might be merciful to him and his congregation and that they would spare their lives and move on. With humbleness, Hassan stood before the Islamist gunmen as He prepared to share his conversion experience with them though in his spirit, he prayed for boldness to share the light of the gospel to those that were living in spiritual darkness.

"In the book of Acts of the Holy Bible the Apostle Paul shared his testimony to fellow Jews who were living in spiritual darkness because they had not yet come to faith in the Lord Jesus Christ," said Hassan. Hassan quoted the Apostle Paul's own words in Acts 22:4-5 "I persecuted the followers of this Way to their death, arresting both men and women and throwing them into prison, as also the high priest and all the Council can testify. I even obtained letters from them to their brothers in Damascus and went there to bring these people as prisoners to Jerusalem to be punished."

"You all personally know how I served Allah with you in hunting down those who became apostates to Islam by converting to Christianity," said Hassan to the Islamist gunmen. "You witnessed me give Christians the opportunity to recant their faith in Jesus of Nazareth under the threat of death though many did not recant," Hassan continued. "And you watched me put to death those who did not recant their faith in Jesus Christ--men, women and children," said Hassan. "Each time I encountered such Christians in these situations I was struck with wonderment of how former Muslims could put such faith in this Jesus, even going to their grave," lamented Hassan. "But I was blinded by the teaching of a god who does not exist, and I was filled with such hate that I boldly and gladly hunted them and killed them," said Hassan.

The Holy Spirit was present as Hassan preached his testimony to his audience consisting of these six-armed Islamist gunmen, his church congregation that he personally evangelized as he told them of the possible risk of such a day as this. And of course, Benjamin, Amnon and the other angels who were watching Hassan intervening for his congregation though they already knew the outcome to be.

Hassan continued sharing the Apostle Paul's testimony of his conversion to faith in Jesus Christ by quoting the Apostle Paul's own words in Acts 22:6-8 "About noon as I came near Damascus, suddenly a bright light from heaven flashed around me. I fell to the ground and heard a voice say to me, "Saul, Saul! Why do you persecute me?"

"Who are you, Lord?"

"I am Jesus of Nazareth whom you are persecuting," he replied.

Hassan shared his own experience of seeing the Lord Jesus Christ in three separate night visions in a row. In each vision the Lord Jesus Christ asked Hassan why he was persecuting Him. Hassan then told everyone that he then repented of his grievous sins and asked Jesus to be merciful to him as he asked Jesus' forgiveness.

Hassan lastly shared the Apostle Paul's commission to preach the gospel message of salvation to the Jews as well as to the Gentiles. Hassan quoted Jesus' words of the Apostle Paul in Acts 26:16-18 "Now get up and stand on your feet. I have appeared to you to appoint you as a servant and as a witness of what you have seen of me and what I will show you. I will rescue you from your own people and from the Gentiles. I am sending you to them to open their eyes and turn them from darkness to light, and from the power of Satan to God, so that they may receive forgiveness of sins and a place among those who are sanctified by faith in me."

"Jesus then informed me to accept His salvation and turn from Islam and preach His saving gospel message to other Afghans," said Hassan. Hassan then pointed to his congregation and said, "You are the fruit of my labor in the ministry of Jesus Christ."

There was a moment of complete silence that had finally replaced the sounds of joy and blessings of worship that was taking place before the six Islamist gunmen burst through the door of that small country church in the remote countryside of Afghanistan. Anticipation began to build as though no one in the barn knew what was going to happen. But of course, Benjamin, Amnon and the other angels knew. This Afghan congregation was their assignment.

CHAPTER SIX

"Is that it, Hassan?" asked one of the gunmen. "Is that all you have to say?" he continued.

"Is that message supposed to make us feel sorry for you and these apostates of Islam?" another of the gunmen asked. "Well, we're not moved," the gunmen continued. "Today we're going to get rid of this church of Jesus followers once and for all," the gunman continued.

Hassan, having previously been a member of this group, pretty much knew what was going to happen. His congregation also had fearful suspicions as well. The women and children began to weep and pray just loud enough to be heard by the gunmen. Hassan tried to encourage his congregation.

"Remember what Jesus told Peter in Matthew 16:18 'And I tell you that you are Peter, and on this rock, I will build my Church, and the gates of Hades will not overcome it.' Brothers and sisters, Jesus also said in Matthew 18:20, 'For where two or three come together in my name, there am I with them,'" continued Hassan.

"Brothers and sisters let us join hands and bow our heads in prayer to our Lord Jesus who is present with us in this place and may the Lord Jesus forgive these men who will carry out Satan's work, though they know not what they are doing," continued Hassan.

As Hassan and his congregation prayed Benjamin prepared the angels for their work. "Angels, stand next to your assignment to catch these faithful believers," said Benjamin to the other angels.

At that moment, the six Islamist gunmen all yelled in unison "In the name of Allah, kill the infidels!"

The Islamist gunmen fired their semi-automatic weapons into the lives of Hassan and his congregation of men, women, and children until their guns were empty. No life was spared. The six gunmen exited the barn and set the barn on fire, burning it to the ground. They then left the area.

On the other side of death's door, the angels were holding in their hands the spirits of Hassan and all the members of his congregation. All family members were still together.

"Welcome!" said Benjamin to Hassan and his congregation. "We are God's holy angels who have the privileged opportunity to serve God in carrying the spirits of deceased Christian believers to heaven," Benjamin joyfully exclaimed.

"We're really going to heaven?" asked a little girl.

Servants of the Most High God

"You sure are," replied Amnon. "And you all are going to see what a beautiful and glorious place it is," continued Amnon.

"Will we see Jesus there?" asked a young boy. "Absolutely!" replied Benjamin. "He'll be right next to your heavenly Father," continued Benjamin.

"We want you all to relax and we will have you there in just a moment," said Amnon.

It only took a moment and Benjamin and Amnon and the other angels had Hassan and his congregation walking through the everlasting open door to heaven. There was the brightness of the glory of God the Father seated on His throne. Next to the Father was Jesus who greeted this church congregation from Afghanistan. For the first time they saw their savior face to face.

"I've been praying for all of you," said Jesus. "Welcome to the Father's house," continued Jesus as He gave each one a heavenly embrace.

In light of Hassan's conversion and ministry he could not help but be appreciative for the salvation he received through Jesus' death on Calvary's Cross. Hassan remembered the words of the Apostle Paul in Romans 5:8, "But, God demonstrates His own love for us in this: while we were still sinners, Christ died for us."

"Thank you for your faithfulness in service," Jesus said to Hassan. "Please, lead your congregation into a time of worship, you are all home now," Jesus continued.

Hassan did just what Jesus encouraged him to do. The last thing he was doing in life this Sunday morning was leading his congregation in worship of God. Now Hassan and his congregation were worshiping in heaven itself and in the presence of the Father and the Son. It was true as Jesus said--they were home.

Benjamin and Amnon entered into worship themselves for a short bit. But they had their next assignment to go to. Being angels, they never tire and their line of service to God is continual. But since they carry the spirits of Christian believers to heaven when they die, it is always a joyful and rewarding experience because the Christian believer goes to an eternal place of bliss.

"Take your last look Amnon until we get back," said Benjamin. "But we have another of God's children to bring home," continued Benjamin.

With that, Benjamin and Amnon sped off to their next assignment.

CHAPTER SEVEN

Marshal

"Amnon, I don't think the average person knows how much God really loves them," said Benjamin, as they sped to their next assignment. "In the realm of man, God often demonstrates His great persistence as well as His great patience in striving to bring sinful man unto His great salvation through His Son, Jesus Christ," Benjamin continued.

"Well Benjamin, as God's holy angels, we have never experienced sin, nor the need to be saved from the penalty of sin," replied Amnon. "But in our observation of God's working with mankind we surely have seen God's persistence and patience bring about saving results," continued Amnon. "Even the Apostle Peter spoke of this very thing in 2nd Peter 3:8-9 when he states 'But do not forget this one thing, dear friends: With the Lord a day is like a thousand years, and a thousand years are like a day. The Lord is not slow in keeping His promise, as some understand slowness. He is patient with you, not wanting anyone to perish, but everyone to come to repentance,'" Amnon went on to say.

"I think Jesus sums the love of God towards mankind as He told Nicodemus in John 3:16, "For God so loved the world that He gave His one and only Son, that whoever believes in Him shall not perish but have eternal life." said Benjamin.

"And so, to encourage those who may question or doubt the validity of being able to receive eternal life through Jesus Christ, the Apostle John declared in 1st John 5:13, 'I write these things to you who believe in the name of the Son of God so that you may know that you have eternal life.'" replied Amnon.

"If only we could testify to people that saving faith in Jesus Christ will allow one to spend eternity in heaven with Jesus," said Benjamin.

"That's what I love about the service God has commissioned us to do, Benjamin, we get to take the spirits of Christian believers to heaven when the Christian believer dies," said Amnon.

"But don't forget Amnon, to God they are His spiritual children," said Benjamin. "And what was God's decree to us in this service?" asked Benjamin.

"Servants of the Most High God, bring my children home!" replied Amnon.

"Where are we headed to for our next assignment? Amnon asked Benjamin.

"We're headed to the country of Germany," replied Benjamin. "But we're going early for this next assignment," continued Benjamin.

"Why are we going early? asked Amnon.

Benjamin was so full of excitement as he asked Amnon "Why do you think?" replied Benjamin. "I really can't believe you even have to ask," continued Benjamin.

Servants of the Most High God

"You mean?" Amnon stopped his question as he thought he might know the answer as he swelled with excitement also.

"That's right!" exclaimed Benjamin. "Our next assignment is still an unbeliever, and we get to watch the Holy Spirit of God at work as we watch the Holy Spirit bring this unbeliever to saving faith in Jesus Christ before He dies," Benjamin continued.

"Now that is so characteristic of the God we serve, Benjamin!" Exclaimed Amnon. "He truly desires none to perish but all come to repentance," continued Amnon.

And God is so good to give us the opportunity to watch the One who created all of the universe recreate a sinful man into a redeemed man, washed and cleansed through the blood of Jesus," replied Benjamin. "I can't wait to see the results," continued Benjamin.

"Me too!" exclaimed Amnon.

CHAPTER EIGHT

    Benjamin and Amnon arrived early in the morning of the last day of the German Shepherd Dog World Sieger Show in Germany. It was the day of the working dog class competing for the honorable and prestigious title of World Sieger. Marshal and Jim were two men from the United States who lived in different areas of the country but had met here a few days before to watch this very prestigious show.
    Marshal was a man in his 50's who was a very respected and successful breeder of German Shepherd Dogs of German show lines. He had come to this most prestigious show because he was in the market for buying the best male dog, he could for his breeding kennel in Houston, Texas. Jim was a church pastor in his 50's as well and was from the state of Pennsylvania. Jim had bought a female German Shepherd puppy from Marshal two years earlier. Jim was an invitee of Marshal because of a future breeding Marshal wanted to do with Jim's dog. Marshal and Jim had spent a considerable amount of time talking with one another the few days they were in Germany and were quite comfortable with one another. Marshal, a businessman, was always meeting people in his kennel business and oftentimes hosting business parties at

his home. Jim, a church pastor, likewise was always dealing with people inside and outside of the church. Benjamin and Amnon were not at the dog show to watch the dogs. Instead, they were there to watch the Holy Spirit bring Marshal, an unbelieving sinner, to faith in Jesus Christ through repentance of his sins. The Holy Spirit would accomplish this today before Marshal leaves this life through the death that has been appointed for him. Marshal and Jim were not aware of God's plan to bring Marshal to saving faith though Jim would have a part to play in the accomplishment of God's plan.

      Both Marshal and Jim took their seats as they settled in to watch the climax of the dog show. There were exhibitors and spectators from all around the world, though most were from Germany. Marshal was at the show with the intention to buy a dog and Jim was there as an invited guest of Marshal.

      "I see you're quite serious about your dogs, Marshal," said Jim.

      "You better believe it," replied Marshal. "To be truthful, this is what my life is all about, Jim," replied Marshal. "I don't have anything else, or anyone else for that matter in my life, Jim," continued Marshal. "My wife and kids left me. My wife then divorced me, and my kids won't talk to me," Marshal went on to say.

      "Have you tried reaching out to them?" Jim asked.

      "Oh, sure, but it does no good, none of them want anything to do with me," replied Marshal.

      "Do you have any friends, Marshal?" asked Jim.

      "You mean people I can trust in, count on, or confide with?" asked Marshal.

      "Yes, that's right," replied Jim.

"I have a lot of acquaintances, but no true friends," replied Marshal. "To be truthful Jim, I'm actually quite lonely a lot of the time," said Marshal. "On the weekends I often hold parties for my so-called friends and business acquaintances, both men and women," continued Marshal.

"I can honestly say that I feel your pain, Marshal." replied Jim.

"I smoke a lot, I drink a lot, I use bad and profane language a lot, I sometimes do a little drugs at the parties," lamented Marshal. "Sometimes I gamble--at the card tables, on sports games, at the track, and now and then I gamble in sin city--Vegas," said Marshal. "Do you still feel my pain?" Asked Marshal.

"I do," replied Jim. "And I want you to know I care," continued Jim.

During the conversation Marshal and Jim were having, the dog show continued to move right along. Because of the conversation, Marshal was not even watching what he had travelled such a long distance to see. To Marshal, the world just seemed to consist of himself and Jim, and of course all his problems.

"You ready to hear the worst of it, Jim?" Marshal asked.

"What's that?" asked Jim, though he had no idea what he was about to hear next.

"I put my whole life into these dogs, Jim," said Marshal. "But these dogs don't enhance the condition of my life, they don't make life better for me, they don't give me what I really need," continued Marshal.

"And what is that you really need, Marshal?" asked Jim.

Servants of the Most High God

"Love and friendship," replied Marshal. "I'm tired of being lonely and always feeling like no one really cares about me," lamented Marshal.

"Marshal, there are many people in the world who try to fill their lives with all kinds of things, just like you are doing, hoping it will satisfy their souls," said Jim. "What you and they need is a relationship with Jesus Christ," continued Jim.

Benjamin and Amnon were seat side with Marshal and Jim, observing the presence and ministry of the Holy Spirit.

"Amnon, do you remember what Jesus said of the presence and ministry of the Holy Spirit in John 16:8? Asked Benjamin.

"He said, "When He (the Holy Spirit) comes, He will convict the world of guilt regarding sin and righteousness and judgement:" replied Amnon.

"Marshal is experiencing the results of a sinful lifestyle, and who's feeling the pain of brokenness and despair," said Benjamin. "And on top of that he thinks no one cares," said Benjamin. "He doesn't know he's going to die today but God knows, and so do we because that's why we are here," Benjamin went on to say.

"God is demonstrating that He cares enough to continue pursuing Marshal, exercising His eternal patience because He desires none to perish, including Marshal," said Amnon. "For the moment, the Holy Spirit has caused Marshal to reflect on his spiritual needs which are greater than his dog interests," continued Amnon.

"Not only that, but the Holy Spirit arranged for Marshal to invite a church pastor along on the trip not only to listen to Marshal but also to share the gospel message of salvation to Marshal, said Benjamin.

"The Apostle Paul said in Romans 10:17 "Consequently, faith comes from hearing the message, and the message is heard through the word of Christ," said Amnon.

"You know Marshal, you are experiencing a life spiritually separated from God due to sin in your life," said Jim. "But don't think you are all alone in this condition," continued Jim. "The Bible states in Romans 3:23 "for all have sinned and fall short of the glory of God," Jim went on to say.

"Are you telling me that every other human being that has ever lived has sinned?" asked Marshal.

"That's what that verse of scripture is saying, Marshal," replied Jim. "But over the years you have allowed sin to take over much of your life as you have described your life to me, Marshal. Let me share with you how the Apostle Paul declares the expression of the sinful nature," continued Jim. "In Galatians 5:19-21 the Apostle Paul states, "The acts of the sinful nature are obvious: sexual immorality, impurity and debauchery; idolatry and witchcraft; hatred, discord, jealousy, fits of rage, selfish ambition, dissensions, factions and envy; drunkenness, orgies, and the like. I warn you, as I did before, that those who live like this will not inherit the kingdom of god."

Marshal was now beginning to feel guilty of his sinfulness and was beginning to see how the sin in his life was ruining his life. He wanted to be free of the burdensome life he was living, and he wanted to start life over.

Servants of the Most High God

"Jim, how do I get rid of this sin that has taken over my life, please tell me you know the answer," pleaded Marshal.

Jim was now greatly aware not only of the presence of the Holy Spirit, but he was also realizing that the Holy Spirit had intentionally had Marshal invite him to this show. Jim was believing that the Holy Spirit had spiritually and miraculously arranged this encounter for the salvation of Marshal's soul.

CHAPTER NINE

Benjamin and Amnon had been patient in their observance of the Holy Spirit at work in the lives of Marshal and Jim. The Holy Spirit knew the words Marshal needed to hear and He was bringing those words to Marshal's hearing as He guided Jim in the words to share. And yet Benjamin and Amnon were building an excitement as they anticipated the Holy Spirit bringing Marshal to faith in Jesus Christ. Since Marshal was their assignment, they knew this was a done deal, Jesus Himself declared in Luke 15:10 "In the same way, I tell you, there is rejoicing in the presence of the angels of God over one sinner who repents."

"Marshal, I have good news to tell you!" exclaimed Jim. "The Apostle Paul states in Romans 5:8 'But God demonstrates His own love for us in this: while we were still sinners, Christ died for us,'" continued Jim.
Marshal, feeling a state of desperation asked Jim, "What must I do to be saved from my sins?"
"The first thing to know, Marshal, is there's nothing you can do to bring about your salvation," replied Jim. "In fact, the Apostle Paul states in Ephesians 2:8-9 'For it is by grace you have been saved, through faith--and this not from

yourselves, it is the gift of God--not by works, so that no one can boast,'" continued Jim. Jim went on to tell Marshal the words of the Apostle Paul in Romans 10:9, "That if you confess with your mouth, 'Jesus is Lord,' and believe in your heart that God raised Him from the dead, you will be saved."

"Jim, I believe in all that you're telling me," said Marshal. "Can I receive forgiveness of my sins today, even right now?" asked Marshal.

Absolutely! Exclaimed Jim. "Let me lead you in prayer," continued Jim.

Jim led Marshal in prayer as Marshal acknowledged to Jesus, he was a sinner and needed His forgiveness and cleansing of his sins. Marshal asked Jesus to come into his life as his Savior and Lord.

"Am I truly forgiven and cleansed of all my sins now?" Marshall asked Jim.

"As the Apostle John states in 1st John 1:9 "If we confess our sins, He is faithful and just and will forgive us our sins and purify us from all unrighteousness," replied Jim. "It's a done deal," said Jim.

"What about changing my life?" asked Marshal.

"Marshal, your life will change," replied Jim. "Let me tell you why," continued Jim. "The Apostle Paul says in Galatians 5:22-23, 'But the fruit of the Spirit is love, joy, peace, patience, kindness, goodness, faithfulness, gentleness, and self-control. Against such things there is no law,'" Jim went on to say.

"Can you excuse me, Jim?" asked Marshal. "I have a couple of quick phone calls I want to make. I want to give some apologies to a few people as well as to tell them of my brand-new life in Jesus," continued Marshal.

"No problem, Marshal--take your time, I'll be right here," replied Jim.

Marshal walked a short distance away to have some privacy as he made his calls. Jim took the time to pray and give thanks to God for the privilege of sharing the gospel message of salvation to Marshal which resulted in Marshal coming to faith in Jesus Christ. Benjamin and Amnon were dancing for joy for having witnessed Marshal come into the family of God through his faith in Jesus. Marshal was now one of God's children.

"You ready, Amnon?' asked Benjamin.
"I'm ready!" replied Amnon.

Suddenly Marshal dropped to the ground. Jim and other people at the show rushed over to check on Marshal. The EMTs checked Marshal and confirmed he showed no signs of life. The EMTs performed CPR as they rushed Marshal to the hospital but to no avail. Marshal had just exited this life with no warning due to a massive heart attack. Marshal's spirit had just gone through death's door and was now in the hands of Benjamin and Amnon.

"Welcome!" said Benjamin and Amnon. We are two of God's holy angels who, because of your newfound faith in Jesus Christ, are going to carry your spirit to heaven where you will personally meet Jesus," said Benjamin.
"You telling me that I'm not going to the other place?" asked Marshal.
"No way!" exclaimed Amnon. "No doubt about it though, with the sinful lifestyle you were living you were on your way there," continued Amnon. "But God has once again showed how much He truly loves sinful man and that

He truly does not desire anyone to go to that other place," Amnon went on to say.

"But it was your choice to make," said Benjamin. "And you made the right choice by accepting God's salvation through His Son, Jesus Christ," continued Benjamin. "Revelation 21:8 says, 'But the cowardly, the unbelieving, the vile, the murderers, the sexually immoral, those who practice magic arts, the idolaters and all liars-- their place will be in the fiery lake of burning sulfur. This is the second death,' Benjamin went on to say.

"Marshal, we want you to just relax, and we'll have you in heaven in just a moment," said Amnon.
It only took a moment and Marshal was standing at the ever-open door leading into heaven. Not having been a church goer nor having experienced any form of worshipping God, yet Marshal was witnessing visually and audibly the worship of God going on in heaven. And there was Jesus, standing in front of him with a smile and arms opened wide.

"Welcome home, Marshal," as Jesus gave Marshal a heavenly embrace. "I've been praying a long time for your salvation," continued Jesus. "Please, enter into worship and feel at home, you'll have no problems here," Jesus went on to say.

Once again Benjamin and Amnon entered into worship before they left for their next assignment. To them it always gives them great joy in bringing God's children home. When the spirits of Christian believers go to heaven and enter into the very presence of God the Father and Jesus, the Son, they for sure know how much God loves them. After a time of worshipping the God of the universe, seated on His majestic throne, Benjamin and Amnon were on their way to their next assignment. As the holy angels of God, they always serve faithfully, obediently, and joyfully.

CHAPTER TEN

Jonathan

"Amnon, we both have expressed our great joy to serve God in the capacity we do," said Benjamin. But it is not a pretty sight watching mankind suffer all that they do-- physically, emotionally, spiritually, socially, materially, financially and any other way when life does not go well for them," continued Benjamin.

"I know what you mean," replied Amnon. "I feel for them, but we angels cannot empathize with man because we were created differently and serve God differently," continued Amnon. "No doubt about it, Benjamin, the earthly life can be filled with heartache, pain, despair, and at times seemingly hopelessness," Amnon went on to say.

"But it hasn't always been that way," said Benjamin. "Do you remember when God created everything in the universe in six days--and what did God say?" asked Benjamin.

"It is good!" exclaimed Amnon.

Rick Stem

"Do you remember what God said after He created man and in His own image at that, Amnon?" asked Benjamin.

"God said it was very good!" replied Amnon. "And for a time, God had fellowship with man and woman in the Garden of Eden and all was great!" continued Amnon.

"Man was not created to get sick, grow old and die, Amnon." said Benjamin. "But then Satan, working through the serpent, entered the Garden of Eden and changed all that," continued Benjamin. "The fall of man not only affected mankind, but all of creation," said Benjamin. "So much that the Apostle Paul states in Roman 8:22, 'We know that the whole creation has been groaning as in the pains of childbirth right up to the present time,'" continued Benjamin.

"Because of sin, God cursed everything and now man is prone to getting sick, growing old, and dying physically and spiritually," said Amnon. "And on top of that all men are born with the nature to sin," continued Amnon. "And God could not let that lie--He needed to redeem sinful man," Amnon went on to say.

"God chose His Son, Jesus, to redeem sinful man, Amnon," said Benjamin. "Jesus will not only restore sinful man's relationship to God, but the time will come when He will restore the whole earthly world as when God first created it!" exclaimed Benjamin.

"Praise be to Jesus!" exclaimed Amnon. "It is because of sinful man's receiving forgiveness and cleansing of sins that we enjoy our service to God in carrying the spirits of deceased Christian believers to heaven," continued Amnon.

"Servants of the Most High God, bring my children home!" shouted Benjamin and Amnon simultaneously, as they repeated God's commissioning decree to them.

Servants of the Most High God

"But for now, the earthly world that man lives in is Satan's domain," said Benjamin. "And Satan's world is an evil spiritual world, where he and his demons are invisible to man as the Apostle Paul states in Ephesians 6:12 "For our struggle is not against flesh and blood, but against the rulers, against the authorities, against the powers of this dark world and against the spiritual forces of evil in the heavenly realms," continued Benjamin.

"Unless one knows of Satan's nature, character and the ways he works as revealed in God's word, people will not recognize his presence and activities even in people's midst," said Amnon. "With Satan and his demons continually working their evil ways in this world against mankind how can there not be anything but suffering and death?" asked Amnon.

"But God, the sovereign and ruling creator of the universe and whom we joyfully serve faithfully and obediently provides the answer for the sufferers of this world--His Son, Jesus," said Benjamin. "Listen to Jesus' own words in Luke 4:18, 'The Spirit of the Lord is on me, because He has anointed me to preach good news to the poor. He has sent me to proclaim freedom for the prisoners and recovery of sight for the blind, to release the oppressed, to prepare the year of the Lord's favor,'" continued Benjamin.

CHAPTER ELEVEN

Approaching their next assignment Benjamin reminds Amnon of the busy year they have had in the year of the world-wide Covid-19 pandemic. Millions of people have died because of the virus, but there were many thousands who died as Christian believers, therefore keeping Benjamin and Amnon busy throughout the year of 2020.

"Amnon, when you think about the Covid-19 pandemic, we have been very busy taking God's children home!" exclaimed Benjamin. "To be truthful though, most people have no idea that we have been as busy as we have been," said Benjamin.

"You know who contributed to that, don't you, Benjamin?" asked Amnon.

"Let me guess--our former worship leader, Lucifer, I mean Satan?" asked Benjamin.

"You got it--our former worship leader who wanted to be God," replied Amnon.

"Satan used the Covid-19 virus to come against God's children," said Benjamin. "Through an unbelieving world he pushed the message of its spreading which included an inability to stop it," continued Benjamin.

Servants of the Most High God

"Yeah, and he spread a message that everyone would sooner or later contract the virus--creating a great FEAR in everyone he could, including God's children," Amnon replied. "Satan pushed a message of death, which elevated that message of FEAR," continued Amnon.

"And the one purpose, we angels and mankind were created alike, is that we were created to WORSHIP our great God and creator," said Benjamin. "But working with the Covid-19 virus through an unbelieving world Satan found a way to bring the corporate worship of God's children to a halt," lamented Benjamin.

"Under the guise of safety and welfare he found a way to close churches, whether by force or voluntarily, so God's children were unable to gather together in brotherly fellowship and ministry to one another," lamented Amnon. "And yet the author of Hebrews encourages God's children to come together as stated in Hebrews 10:24-25, 'And let us consider how we may spur one another on toward love and good deeds. Let us not give up meeting together, as some are in the habit of doing, but let us encourage one another--and all the more as you see the Day approaching,'" Amnon went on to say.

"All year long Satan has been strutting himself throughout the world always striving to create FEAR for everyone, including God's children," said Benjamin. "The Apostle Peter describes him well in 1st Peter 5:8 'Be self-controlled and alert. Your enemy the devil prowls around like a roaring lion looking for someone to devour,'" continued Benjamin.

"Yeah, Satan definitely acts like a bully, Benjamin," replied Amnon. "Through the unbelieving world he preached the message of death to intimidate and to cause many to cringe and cower in fear, causing many to suffer anxiety, depression and hopelessness," lamented Amnon. "And through it all, if the world would only turn to Jesus in faith they could go to heaven whenever they do die," continued Amnon.

"Everyone can be encouraged by the words of Hebrews 2:14-15 'Since the children have flesh and blood, He too shared in their humanity so that by His death He might destroy him who holds the power of death--that is, the devil--and free those who all their lives were held in slavery by their fear of death!" exclaimed Benjamin. "But despite the message of death that Satan tried to propagate, not everyone contracted the virus because God's hand of protection was upon them," said Benjamin.

"And there were those who did contract the virus, but God healed them!" exclaimed Amnon.

"We can praise God for the healing that comes through His Son, Jesus," replied Benjamin.

"But for those who did die because of the virus we don't have the answers to anyone but to say God is a sovereign God and a good God at that," said Amnon. "But no doubt about it, we have been very busy this past year," continued Amnon.

"Now we've arrived for our next assignment," said Benjamin.

CHAPTER TWELVE

"Here we are, Amnon, do you remember being here before?" asked Benjamin.

"This is that one hospital in Los Angeles that has a special husband and wife doctor team, right Benjamin?" Asked Amnon in reply.

"Well, if you're thinking of that born again, spirit filled, Christian husband and wife doctor team that have much faith in their Lord and Savior, Jesus Christ, then that's the one," replied Benjamin.

"I tell you, Benjamin, this husband, Dr. Bill, and his wife, Dr. Linda, have gained a reputation in heaven this past year for the number of unbelieving Covid-19 patients they personally led to faith in Jesus Christ," said Amnon. "In fact, we carried a few spirits who died from Covid-19 in this hospital that told us of the great compassion of Jesus that Dr. Bill and Dr. Linda demonstrated while caring for them," continued Amnon. "I remember the spirits telling us after they were in our hands that though Dr. Bill and Dr. Linda were physically and emotionally exhausted at times, the Holy Spirit quickened and empowered these two doctors to share the gospel message of salvation and eternal life with them, and then led them into the sinner's prayer," Amnon went on to say.

Rick Stem

Benjamin and Amnon entered the room that contained their next assignment--an older gentlemen named Jonathan. Jonathan was on a respirator suffering physically because of the Covid-19 virus. And present with him was Dr. Bill, encouraging him with the words of Jesus, before praying with him for the last time. Jonathan then died.

"Welcome!" exclaimed Benjamin. "I am Benjamin, and this is Amnon, we are God's holy angels that are going to carry your spirit to heaven, your eternal home," continued Benjamin.

"So, I finally died," said Jonathan. "And none of my family was with me once I entered the hospital," continued Jonathan. "But look at me now--on my way to heaven, right guys!" exclaimed Jonathan.

"Right!" exclaimed Benjamin and Amnon simultaneously.

"We're taking your spirit to heaven and it'll only take a moment," said Amnon.

"Guys, before we go, I want to tell you something," said Jonathan. "If it wasn't for that Christian husband and wife doctor team who took care of me, you wouldn't be taking me to heaven," continued Jonathan. "Dr. Bill and Dr. Linda showed the love of Jesus with all of their patients," Jonathan went on to say.

"Those two doctors have gained a reputation in heaven," said Benjamin. "Because of their faithfulness to Jesus, in sharing the love and gospel message of Jesus, there are many in heaven right now," continued Benjamin.

"I heard those two doctors praying words of encouragement with Christian believers before they died," said Jonathan. "After hearing those two doctors praying for other patients, I was ready to accept Jesus as my Savior," said Jonathan. "Dr. Bill expressed his apologies for my family, non-believers as they are, for not being able to be with me," Jonathan went on to say.

"Dr. Bill told me that Jesus died for my sins, but that He rose again and is in heaven right now where there is no suffering and death," said Jonathan. "I told Dr. Bill that I wanted Jesus and heaven and he led me into the sinner's prayer," continued Jonathan.

"Well, let's get you there," said Amnon. "Just relax and we'll have you there in just a moment," continued Amnon.

It literally took only a moment, and Benjamin and Amnon were at the ever-open door leading into heaven. Jonathan had not been a church goer, but he found himself in awe of seeing the glory of God in all His majesty and splendor. And then, Jesus was standing before him with arms open wide to give Jonathan a heavenly embrace.

"Welcome home, I've been praying for you," said Jesus. "Please, enter into worship where your sufferings are over," continued Jesus.

Though just becoming a Christian believer moments before he died, Jonathan was experiencing heaven as though he had always been there. In reality, Jonathan was experiencing going from living in the world of Satan's domain to living in God's heaven. Jonathan was now experiencing the words of Revelation 21:4 "He will wipe away every tear from their eyes. There will be no more death or mourning or crying or pain, for the old order of things has passed away."

Although Jonathan's unbelieving family have no way of knowing that he became a Christian believer before he died and his spirit is now in heaven, yet there is always hope for other patients as long as there are born again, spirit filled, Christian doctors and nurses who will share the love of Jesus and the gospel message of salvation with their Covid-19 patients as Drs. Bill and Linda do.

To all others who are living in this world of heartache and suffering they can always turn to Jesus who stated in John 16:33 "I have told you these things, so that in me you may have peace. In this world you will have trouble. But take heart! I have overcome the world."

CHAPTER THIRTEEN

Tim

As Benjamin and Amnon were in route to their next assignment they found themselves discussing a topic that is often hard to understand and sometimes harder to accept, even by the most faithful of God's children--the sovereignty of God.

"Amnon, since our creation we have watched and observed God do all that He does and at times not even we have understood it," said Benjamin. "Even with His children God says in Isaiah 55:8-9, 'For my thoughts are not your thoughts, neither are your ways my ways,'" declares the Lord. "As the heavens are higher than the earth, so are my ways higher than your ways and my thoughts are higher than your thoughts." continued Benjamin.

"No doubt about it, Benjamin, we have witnessed and observed God's doings and we have seen that God always accomplishes what He plans to accomplish," said Amnon. "God said it all in Isaiah 46:9-10, 'Remember the former things, those of long ago; I am God, and there is no other; I am God, and there is none like me. I make known the end from the beginning, from ancient times, what is still to come. I say: My purpose will stand, and I will do all that I please,'" continued Amnon.

"We have watched over and over God's children at times struggle with trying to understand the reasons God does what He does and how He does what he does," said Benjamin. "But we have always seen God fulfill the words spoken by the Apostle Paul in Romans 8:28, 'And we know that in all things God works for the good of those who love Him, who have been called according to His purpose,'" continued Benjamin.

"In our observations of God's dealings with mankind we have seen that nothing changes the attributes of God," said Amnon. "In Malachi 3:6 God said, 'I the Lord do not change,'" said Amnon. "And concerning God's Son, the Lord Jesus Christ, He doesn't change either as stated in Hebrews 13:8 which says, 'Jesus Christ is the same yesterday and today and forever,'" continued Amnon.

"All this makes our next assignment very interesting indeed," said Benjamin.

"Why is that?" asked Amnon.

"Because our next assignment is an individual where many who know him, fellow Christian believers and non-believers alike, have been struggling with the very topic we have been discussing," replied Benjamin. "You see, Amnon, our next assignment is a young pastor of thirty-five years of age who is dying of terminal cancer," said Benjamin.

"What's his name?" asked Amnon.

"His name is Tim," replied Benjamin. "And Tim is of the character that any Christian believer could emulate and by doing so would benefit in their Christian life," continued Benjamin. "Tim is an exemplary husband, father, and pastor," said Benjamin. "Tim truly expresses the fruit of the Spirit in his young life," said Benjamin.

"Galatians 5:22-23 says "But the fruit of the Spirit is love, joy, peace, patience, kindness, goodness, faithfulness, gentleness and self-control. Against such things there is no law," said Amnon. "You mean that Tim has developed all this in his young life already?" asked Amnon.

"That's right Amnon," replied Benjamin.

"How did that happen so quickly?" asked Amnon.

"Because Tim truly loves Jesus and so he has continually yielded himself to the ministry of the Holy Spirit in obedience to the Word of God," replied Benjamin. "Therefore, the Holy Spirit has been conforming Tim into the image of Jesus, His Lord and Savior," said Benjamin.

"But then why would God take Tim home now if he is the epitome of what God would like all of His children to be like?" asked Amnon.

"And that Amnon, is the very question and struggle that all who know Tim have been dealing with," replied Benjamin. "But remember, Amnon, Tim is only a reflection of Jesus--he's not Jesus," said Benjamin. "God wants all of His children to be conformed into the image of His Son, Jesus, not Tim," continued Benjamin.

With all that having been said, Benjamin and Amnon arrive at Tim's home in Texas where family and visitors continue to visit and pray.

CHAPTER FOURTEEN

Benjamin and Amnon arrived at Tim's house unnoticed of course because they are spirits--angels. Tim is under hospice care and in these last days he always has visitors. But it is no wonder as to his always having visitors because he has made such a big and positive impact in other peoples' lives, especially those whom he has regularly ministered to as their pastor. Tim seems to always be there when his spiritual flock is in need. But even though Tim has not yet met Benjamin and Amnon, he is quite aware that according to the scriptures, at the time of his death angels will be present to carry his spirit to heaven where he will always be in the presence of Jesus.

"Amnon, some of these people in this house right now are people that they themselves previously had cancer," said Benjamin. "But Tim was right there with them so to speak," continued Benjamin. "You see, Amnon, Tim truly loves the people he pastors, and he cares about people in general, especially in times of suffering," said Benjamin.
"It sounds as though the love of God fills his life," said Amnon.

Servants of the Most High God

"You can surely say that," replied Benjamin. "But Tim is one who not only delights in studying God's Word, but he delights in proclaiming it as well," said Benjamin. "But more importantly, Tim believes God's word," continued Benjamin.

"As he should," replied Amnon. "The prophet Isaiah characterizes God as a God of truth as he states in Isaiah 65:16, 'Whoever invokes a blessing in the land will do so by the God of truth; he who takes an oath in the land will swear by the God of truth. For the past troubles will be forgotten and hidden from my eyes,'" said Amnon quoting Isaiah. "Jesus Himself declares God's word to be truth as he states in John 17:17, 'Sanctify them by the truth; your word is truth,'" said Amnon quoting Jesus.

"Also, Amnon, Jesus declares Himself to be truth as he states in John 14:6, "Jesus answered, I am the way and the truth and the life. No one comes to the Father but through me," said Benjamin quoting Jesus.

"And the Holy Spirit is also truth as stated in John 16:13, 'But when He, the Spirit of truth, comes, He will guide you into all truth. He will not speak on His own, He will speak only what He hears, and He will tell you what is yet to come,'" continued Amnon quoting Jesus.

"In Tim's pastoral ministry he has proclaimed the word of God, publicly from the pulpit, and privately as he ministered to those in times of suffering," said Benjamin. "In this fallen world which man lives, man is susceptible to sickness and disease, sometimes leading unto death," continued Benjamin. "And being a good and caring pastor Tim has always been there sharing his trust in God and His word, because those dealing with cancer need someone they can trust in to heal them of this deadly disease," continued Benjamin.

"The diagnosis of cancer can immediately grip anyone's attention with a degree of fear, because of how many people die from this deadly disease every year worldwide," said Amnon. "It is a disease that is not limited to any single group of people--age, gender, race, geographical location--it does not discriminate," continued Amnon.

"Tim has seen and experienced the power of prayer and the truth of God's word as he and others prayed for those with cancer and saw God heal them," declared Benjamin. "On those occasions Tim and his church congregation did as the Psalmist did in Psalms 103:2- 3, 'Praise the Lord, oh my soul, and forget not all his benefits--who forgives all your sins and heals all your diseases,'" said Benjamin. "And then the day came when seemingly out of nowhere Tim was informed by the doctor that he had an advanced stage of cancer and an aggressive one at that," said Benjamin.

"And what was Tim's response to the news?" asked Amnon.

"Well, Tim is no different than most people getting such news, it was a shock to say the least," replied Benjamin. "But when the doctor told Tim and his wife that his cancer was terminal and that he only had months to live, it literally took Tim to his knees, the shock was so great," said Benjamin. "Because of Tim's character in being an exemplary Christian believer, a loving husband, a caring father, and pastor--one whose life could be emulated for a man of his young age, from Tim, his wife, his children and his church congregation came the question everyone wanted the answer to--WHY GOD?" continued Benjamin.

"And yet Tim is not alone in this dilemma in dealing with this deadly disease," said Amnon. "Millions of people worldwide everyday are fighting against this deadly disease," continued Amnon.

"But unlike so many people who have not yet experienced the saving love of God through His Son, Jesus,

Servants of the Most High God

Tim had someone ever so close helping him even from the moment of his news," said Benjamin in an almost preachy tone of voice. "Right from the moment of receiving the news of his cancer Tim experienced God's help as the Apostle Paul states in Romans 8:26-27, 'In the same way, the Spirit helps us in our weakness. We do not know what we ought to pray for, but the Spirit Himself intercedes for us with groans that words cannot express. And He who searches our hearts knows the mind of the Spirit, because the Spirit intercedes for the saints in accordance with God's will,'" proclaimed Benjamin.

"Just knowing that the presence and power of the Holy Spirit is at work in Tim's life ought to give anyone hope as we have witnessed many times of the sustaining work, He has done in the lives of Christian believers especially in their most struggling of times," proclaimed Amnon, in an almost preachy tone of voice as well.

"The Holy Spirit reminded Tim of God's love for him as he remembered the words of the Apostle Paul in Romans 5:8 "But God demonstrates His own love for us in this: While we were still sinners Christ died for us," said Benjamin. "As the weeks went by the Holy Spirit led Tim to reflect on that very time of suffering that led Jesus to His crucifixion and death--including dying for Tim," said Benjamin. "The Holy Spirit led Tim to realize the loneliness Jesus experienced during His own time of suffering as stated in Psalm 22:1-2, 'My God, my God, why have you forsaken me? Why are you so far from saving me, so far from the words of my groaning?" lamented Benjamin as he quoted the Psalmist. "Tim was led to feel the pain of the insults of sinful men toward Jesus as stated in Psalm 22:6-8, 'But I am a worm and not a man, scorned by men and despised by the people. All who see me mock me; they hurl insults, shaking their heads: He trusts in the Lord; let the Lord rescue Him, since he delights in Him,'" lamented Benjamin again quoting the Psalmist.

"And we watched it all play out," said Amnon. "Our creator, suffering in the flesh as He gave His life as an atonement for sinful man," continued Amnon. "It was not a pretty sight to see, in fact it was most disheartening," said Amnon.

"The Holy Spirit allowed Tim to identify with Jesus as Jesus endured His physical suffering as stated in Psalm 22:14-18, 'I am poured out like water, all my bones are out of joint. My heart has turned to wax, it has melted away within me. My strength is dried up like a potsherd, and my tongue sticks to the roof of my mouth; you lay me in the dust of death. Dogs have surrounded me; a band of evil men has encircled me; they have pierced my hands and my feet. I can count all my bones; people stare and gloat over me. They divide my garments and cast lots for my clothing,'" lamented Benjamin quoting the Psalmist.

"But even though Tim is on the verge of death he knows that Jesus, His Lord and Savior, can identify with all that he is experiencing and yet Tim likewise knows he can identify with Jesus," said Amnon. "In fact, because of Jesus' suffering Tim knows that physical healing was experienced by some who are in Tim's house today because they all believed in the words of Isaiah 53:4-5, 'Surely, He took up our infirmities and carried our sorrows, yet we considered Him stricken by God, smitten by Him, and afflicted. But He was pierced for our transgressions, He was crushed for our iniquities; the punishment that brought us peace was upon Him, and by His wounds we are healed,'" proclaimed Amnon.

CHAPTER FIFTEEN

Tim was beginning to wane and he began to struggle for breath. Tim's wife and children and parents moved in close and laid hands on him as they began to earnestly pray that Tim's transition from this life into eternity would be a smooth one. Of course, Benjamin and Amnon knew this would be a smooth transition. Benjamin and Amnon all the time experience Christian believers going through death's door as they first go into the hands of the angels carrying their spirits to heaven. Their spirits being carried to heaven by the angels is super quick and then they experience the words of the Apostle Paul who states in 1st Corinthians 2:9, "However as it is written: No eye has seen, no ear has heard, no mind has conceived what God has prepared for those who love Him.

In Tim's suffering as the end of his days drew near, he has trusted in the words of the Apostle Paul in Romans 8:18, "I consider that our present sufferings are not worth comparing with the glory that will be revealed in us." Many who love Tim are still struggling as to the big question so many ask--WHY GOD? For Tim, the indwelling Holy Spirit brought him to the Garden of Gethsemane where once again he could identify with the One who died for him, as he also prayed the words of Jesus in Luke 22:42, "Father, if you are willing, take this cup from me; YET NOT MY WILL, BUT YOURS BE

DONE." Tim quietly and peacefully passed from this life through death's door into the hands of Benjamin and Amnon. Right away Benjamin and Amnon introduced themselves to Tim.

"Hello, Tim, we're Benjamin and Amnon," said Benjamin.
"Wait, don't tell me," interjected Tim. "You are the angels who will carry my spirit to heaven, right?" asked Tim.
"That's correct, I'm impressed," said Amnon.
"Well, I do teach the subject of death for the Christian believer," replied Tim. "I just haven't experienced it yet, until now," said Tim.
"Until now!" exclaimed Benjamin. "And what an experience it will be," said Benjamin.
"Is it really as great as the scriptures declare?" asked Tim.
"Better!" exclaimed Amnon. "You see Tim. heaven is truly beyond man's ability to describe it," continued Amnon. "As the author of Hebrews states in chapter 11:16 of those living by faith said, 'Instead, they were longing for a better country--a heavenly one. Therefore, God is not ashamed to be called their God, for He has prepared a city for them,'" continued Amnon.
"Well, guys I'm looking forward to experiencing it!" exclaimed Tim.
"Okay then, Tim, just relax and we'll have you there in just a moment," said Amnon.

Seemingly just like that, Benjamin and Amnon were at heaven's always open door with Tim excited as to what he was about to see and experience. As he entered heaven, right away he realized it was truly greater than his understanding of the scriptures' description of heaven. It was genuinely like another country than the world he just left. The glory of the Father sitting on His throne was most brilliant and the choir of heavenly worship was unlike anything he experienced in any church setting. But then, the One who had made this experience all possible was standing before him with arms open wide--Jesus.

"Welcome home, Tim," Jesus said as He gave Tim a heavenly embrace. "I've been praying for you," continued Jesus.

"Thank you, Lord," replied Tim. "In reading the scriptures concerning your suffering I felt as though I was there with you though I wasn't," said Tim.

"But I was with you in your suffering," replied Jesus. "But all that's over, Tim, there is no suffering here, nor for ever more," said Jesus. "Please, enter into worship," Jesus said in a most encouraging way.

Benjamin and Amnon participated in worship with Tim before they departed for their next assignment. Tim had experienced the sovereignty of God in that though God can and does heal people of sickness and disease, including cancer, God instead chose to not heal Tim and instead take Tim home. Tim trusted his heavenly Father's sovereignty and now he was eternally worshiping God in His heavenly presence.

CHAPTER SIXTEEN

Unnamed

    Benjamin and Amnon once again departed from the most glorious place in all of God's great creation--heaven. There is no place in the entire universe that can compare with it. It is the place where Almighty God sovereignly rules His creation. It is a place that is holy and eternal because God Himself is holy and eternal. And for those who believe in Jesus Christ, His Son, and by faith receive His great salvation, they too will dwell there after death. Benjamin and Amnon and all the rest of God's holy angels have dwelt there since their creation.

    But Benjamin and Amnon conduct their service to God in man's world--the earthly world where God placed man after creating him. Genesis 2:7 states "the Lord God formed the man from the dust of the ground and breathed into his nostrils the breath of life, and the man became a living being." Genesis 2:15 states "The Lord God took the man and put him in the Garden of Eden to work it and take care of it." It was after that, that things went downhill for man.

Servants of the Most High God

"Amnon, do you remember the tranquil environment Adam and Eve lived in before Satan entered the picture?" asked Benjamin.

"I remember it quite well," replied Amnon. "It was physically beautiful and perfect," continued Amnon. "It was a place where God had fellowship with Adam and Eve because there wasn't any sin," said Amnon.

"It was a hard thing to watch Adam and Eve yield to the temptation of Satan, who truly took advantage of them in their state of innocence," said Benjamin. "But Adam and Eve were no match for him as he persuaded them to voluntarily disobey God bringing about their sin and loss of fellowship with God," continued Benjamin. "But long before that Satan persuaded one third of God's holy angels to also disobey God which resulted in God expelling them from His holy heaven," said Amnon. "In fact, Revelation 12:4 states "His tail swept a third of the stars out of the sky and flung them to the earth," continued Amnon.

"And now the earthly world is Satan's domain," said Benjamin. "The Apostle Paul refers to him as the god of this age as he states in 2nd Corinthians 4:4 "The god of this age has blinded the minds of unbelievers, so that they cannot see the light of the gospel of the glory of Christ, who is the image of God," continued Benjamin.

"And sadly, the earthly world is a place of spiritual darkness, great spiritual darkness," said Amnon. "The Apostle Paul describes this great spiritual darkness in Ephesians 6:12 by saying "For our struggle is not against flesh and blood, but against the rulers, against the authorities, against the powers of this dark world and against the spiritual forces of evil in the heavenly realms," continued Amnon.

"But our great creator God provided a way to rescue lost souls out of that spiritual darkness," said Benjamin. "Listen to the Apostle John's words concerning Jesus' coming into this spiritually dark world as stated in John 1:1-5 "In the beginning was the Word, and the Word was with God, and the Word was God. He was with God in the beginning. Through Him all things were made; without Him nothing was made that has been made. In Him was life, and that life was the light of men. The light shines in the darkness, but the darkness has not understood it," continued Benjamin.

"Let me take it from here, Benjamin," said Amnon. "The Apostle John went on to say in John 1:10-14 "He was in the world, and though the world was made through Him, the world did not recognize Him. He came to that which was His own, but His own did not receive Him. Yet to all who received Him, to those who believed in His name, He gave the right to become children of God--children born not of natural descent, nor of human decision or a husband's will, but born of God," continued Amnon.

"And we carry the spirits of these children of God home to their heavenly Father in heaven after they die!" exclaimed Benjamin. "And I love serving God in this capacity!" continued Benjamin.

"Me too, Benjamin!" exclaimed Amnon.

CHAPTER SEVENTEEN

Benjamin and Amnon were arriving at their next destination for their next assignment. Their destination was in the metropolis of New York City. It is a city abounding with human life and activity. It is termed "the city that never sleeps." It is a city of concrete sidewalks, asphalt roads, skyscrapers seemingly reaching to the clouds and lights that never quit shining. And even at night from high in the sky the city is visible because of all the lights. But spiritually it is dark because it is part of Satan's domain and sin abounds. And there are specific locations that are very dark, spiritually.

"Amnon, in the earthly world of sinful man, I don't know if it can get any spiritually darker than in this abortion clinic," lamented Benjamin. "We have been in these places before, but it is still such a dark place to come to," continued Benjamin.
"I feel the same way, Benjamin," said Amnon. "Look at this mother who does not know God nor His Son, Jesus, and who does not look at her developing baby within her as God looks at her baby," said Benjamin. "She knows

Rick Stem

her baby is there but places no individual value of life on her baby but thinks only of herself," continued Benjamin.

"Well, there's also the doctor and the doctor's assistant who also don't know God nor His Son, Jesus, and who likewise places no individual value of life on the mother's developing baby," said Amnon. "And everybody involved is supported by politicians who also don't know God nor His Son, Jesus, but have legislated to make abortion legal," continued Amnon.

"But don't forget all the citizens who not only vote these abortion legislators into office but also send their tax dollars to fund this practice," said Benjamin. "Surely these individuals cannot know God nor His Son, Jesus, so that they would support such a practice," continued Benjamin.

"But each developing baby is known completely by God," said Amnon. "Listen to the words of the Psalmist in Psalm 139:13-16, 'For you created my inmost being you knit me together in my mother's womb. I praise you because I am fearfully and wonderfully made; your works are wonderful; I know that full well. My frame was not hidden from you when I was made in the secret place. When I was woven together in the depths of the earth, your eyes saw my unformed body. All the days ordained for me were written in your book before one of them came to be,'" said Amnon quoting the Psalmist.

"Also, Amnon, don't forget what God told the prophet Jeremiah in Jeremiah 1:5 "Before I formed you in the womb, I knew you, before you were born I set you apart; I appointed you as a prophet to the nations," said Benjamin as he quoted the words of Jeremiah.

"So, not only does God know every human being conceived in the womb of a woman but God is actually involved in that conception?" asked Amnon.

"That's correct, God is an awesome God!" exclaimed Benjamin.

Servants of the Most High God

"It's hard to believe that mothers would destroy the lives of such innocent human beings who are in reality their own children," lamented Amnon.

"Well, Amnon, you and I know who is behind it all--Satan," said Benjamin. "Satan even wanted to take the life of the incarnate Son of God, who was not only to redeem Israel from her sins and restore her relationship with God, but the entire sinful world," said Benjamin. "Listen to the words of the Apostle John as he describes Satan's desire to take the life of God's redeeming Son, Jesus, even at His birth as stated in Revelation 12:1-6, 'A great and wondrous sign appeared in heaven: a woman clothed with the sun, with the moon under her feet and a crown of twelve stars on her head. She was pregnant and cried out in pain as she was about to give birth. Then another sign appeared in heaven: an enormous red dragon with seven heads and ten horns and seven crowns on his heads. His tail swept a third of the stars out of the sky and flung them to the earth. The dragon stood in front of the woman who was about to give birth, so that he might devour her child the moment it was born. She gave birth to a son, a male child, who will rule all the nations with an iron scepter. And her child was snatched up to God and to His throne,'" continued Benjamin.

"And here we are, sitting in this abortion clinic room witnessing Satan take the very life of an unborn child," lamented Amnon. "Through the abortion procedure Satan no longer has to wait for a child to be born but he can now enter into the God-given domain of that developing unborn child and snatch the life away of one who is utterly defenseless," continued Amnon. "No wonder Jesus refers to Satan as a murderer in John chapter eight," said Amnon.

"As I said, Amnon, these places are so spiritually dark for me," lamented Benjamin. "Though this young baby is not known, unnamed, and unwanted it is about to meet their loving Father in heaven," said Benjamin.

CHAPTER EIGHTEEN

Benjamin and Amnon watched as Satan worked through the doctor performing the abortion which resulted in the taking of the young life from its mother who was giving the doctor the permission to do so. Only God would hear the cry of the young life who would be entering through death's door but who would experience the eternal life of the redeemed. This young life would experience the very cry of the Psalmist, David, in Psalm 139:7-10 "Where can I go from your Spirit? Where can I flee from your presence? If I go up to the heavens you are there; if I make my bed in the depths, you are there. If I rise on the wings of the dawn, if I settle on the far side of the sea, even there your hand will guide me, your right hand will hold me fast."

"Welcome!" said Benjamin to the un-named life who was just delivered into Benjamin and Amnon's hands. "I am Benjamin and this is Amnon and we are two of God's holy angels who are going to carry your spirit to heaven where you will meet your heavenly Father and His Son who died for you," continued Benjamin.

"More precisely, we are servants of the Most High God and we take God's children home to Him after they die," said Amnon.

"And you are unique in the family of God," said Benjamin. "No one has named you but that is no problem to God for it is stated in Psalm 147:4, 'He determines the number of the stars, and He calls them each by name,'" continued Benjamin.

"And though no one wanted you from your mother's womb you are most wanted by your Father in heaven as spoken by Jesus in Mathew 19:14, 'Jesus said, Let the little children come to me, and do not hinder them, for the kingdom of heaven belongs to such as these,'" said Amnon.

"And though you have not yet committed sin, yet it was necessary that Jesus died for your sins as stated by the Psalmist, David, as he stated in Psalm 51:5, 'Surely I was sinful at birth, sinful from the time my mother conceived me,'" said Benjamin as he quoted the Psalmist. "Like all men, even you need the salvation of God provided through His Son, Jesus, as stated by the Apostle Paul in Roman's 5:12, 'Therefore, just as sin entered the world through one man, and death through sin, and in this way, death came to all men, because all sinned,' continued Benjamin.

"When will I meet my Father in heaven?" asked the un-named spirit.

"We can take you right now," said Amnon. "Just relax and we'll have you there in just a moment," continued Amnon.

It literally only took a moment and Benjamin and Amnon were at heaven's ever open door with another of God's children with no previous name. As with every human that enters into heaven it is indescribable, just the beauty and gloriousness of it. But in reality, it is all that this child of God with no name has experienced. But God the Father would name him.

Next to God the Father who was sitting on His throne in utmost glory was the One, the Son of God, the Savior of all who place faith in His dying for their sins, Jesus. As Jesus stood there with open arms the new named child of God saw the Father while looking at Jesus, the Son, as stated in Hebrews 1:3, "The Son is the radiance of God's glory and exact representation of His being, sustaining all things by His powerful word. After He had provided purification for sins, He sat down at the right hand of majesty in heaven."

"Are you, my Father?" asked the new named child of God.

Jesus answered the new named child of God by saying what He once told His disciples in John 14:7 "If you really knew me, you would know my Father as well. From now on, you do know Him and have seen Him," "Welcome home, child," said Jesus.

"Abba, Father," replied the new child of God.

This new child of God had just experienced in his very short lifespan of not being known, not being named, not being wanted, and having his physical life taken from him all by the workings of Satan (no fault of his own), to being rescued, redeemed, and restored to someone most loved and fully known by God and all of God's other children in heaven. He would now live the eternal experience of Romans 8:16-17 "The Spirit Himself testifies with our spirit that we are God's children. Now if we are children, then we are heirs--heirs of God and co-heirs with Christ, if indeed we share in His sufferings in order that we may also share in His glory."

Benjamin, Amnon, and the new child of God entered into worship of Him seated on His throne and His Son, Jesus with the angels and other redeemed men, women and children that were also in heaven.

CHAPTER NINETEEN

Sarah

As Benjamin and Amnon are in route to their next assignment they reflect on God's creation of man, but specifically highlighting on the creation of the woman. It happens to be that their next assignment is a woman--an elderly and God-fearing Christian believer who has lived an exemplary Christian life and who has done much to minister to girls and other women throughout her lifetime concerning God and the relationship women and girls can have with Him.

"Amnon, do you remember what it was like when God created man and woman?" asked Benjamin.

"I surely do, it was exciting to see God create a fleshly being yet in His own image so that God could have fellowship with His creation," said Amnon. "In Genesis 1:26 "Then God said, 'Let us make man in our own image, in our likeness, and let them rule over the fish of the sea and the birds of the air, over the livestock, over all the earth, and over all the creatures that move along the ground,'" continued Amnon. "Genesis 1:27 'So God created man in His own image, in the image of God He created him; male and female He created them,'" said Amnon.

"Specifically, we see in Genesis 2:7 "the Lord God formed the man from the dust of the ground and breathed into his nostrils the breath of life, and the man became a living being," said Benjamin. "It was awesome to see the creation of man come about, formed from the ground," continued Benjamin.

"But after all of God's glorious creation had come about, He saw that He needed to put a finishing touch on His creation of man," said Amnon. "Genesis 2:18 'The Lord God said, 'It is not good for man to be alone. I will make a helper suitable for him,'" continued Amnon.

"Just as we thought it was amazing how God created man from the ground, it was just as amazing to watch how He created the woman," said Benjamin. "In Genesis 2:21-22 'So the Lord God caused the man to fall into a deep sleep; and while he was sleeping, He took one of the man's ribs and closed up the place with flesh. Then the Lord God made a woman from the rib He had taken out of the man, and He brought her to the man,'" continued Benjamin.

"It not only shows the amazement of God's creative powers but that he doesn't create anything less than perfection," said Amnon. "God created the woman to "complete" the man according to all his needs-- intellectually, emotionally, physically, and spiritually," continued Amnon.

"Even the man recognized the completeness of him as he states in Genesis 2:23, 'The man said, 'This is now bone of my bones and flesh of my flesh; she shall be called woman, for she was taken out of man,'" said Benjamin. Benjamin went on to state from Genesis 2:24 "For this reason a man will leave his father and mother and be united to his wife, and they will become one flesh," said Benjamin.

"And God gave the man and the woman an especially important commission as stated in Genesis 1:28, 'God blessed them and said to them, 'Be fruitful and increase in number; fill the earth and subdue it. Rule over the fish of the sea and the birds of the air and over every living creature that moves on the ground,'" said Amnon.

"In Genesis 2:15-17, 'The Lord God took the man and put him in the Garden of Eden to work it and take care of it. And the Lord God commanded the man, 'You are free to eat from any tree in the garden; but you must not eat from the tree of the knowledge of good and evil, for when you eat of it you will surely die,'" said Benjamin.

"For certain, God warned the man," said Amnon.

"And when tempted by the serpent to eat from that tree even the woman replied in Genesis 3:2-3, 'The woman said to the serpent, We may eat fruit from the trees in the garden, but God did say, 'You must not eat fruit from the tree that is in the middle of the garden, and you must not touch it, or you will die,' " continued Benjamin.

"But after much lying, deceiving and tempting we watched the woman play right into the wiles of the serpent and disobey God anyway," lamented Amnon.

"Sad to say, but yes she did," said Benjamin. "In Genesis 3:6, 'When the woman saw that the fruit of the tree was good for food and pleasing to the eye, and desirable for gaining wisdom, she took some and ate it. She also gave some to her husband, who was with her, and he ate it.'"

"And God was true to His word," said Amnon. "Because of the woman and the man disobeying God which resulted in sin, God cursed everything, including telling the man in Genesis 3:19 for dust you are and to dust you will return (you will die)," continued Amnon.

"Pertaining to the creation of the woman (and man) from God's perspective, through the centuries the woman and man proved they could not be faithful to God in their relationship with Him or one another," said Benjamin. "The prophet Jeremiah said it well in Jeremiah 17:9, 'The heart is deceitful above all things and beyond cure. Who can understand it?'" continued Benjamin.

"But because of His love for His creation (sinful man) God has always raised up and called men and women to serve Him in proclaiming the gospel message of salvation," said Amnon.

"And it is to this very message that our next assignment has devoted much of her life to," said Benjamin. "She has throughout her life shared the Biblical account of God's creation of woman, and the very special and important role that women are to live," said Benjamin. "Sarah conducted a teaching ministry so she could help other girls and women see their true identity and purpose in life from God's perspective," continued Benjamin.

"I am most eager to meet her!" exclaimed, Amnon.
"Me too!" exclaimed Benjamin.

CHAPTER TWENTY

Benjamin and Amnon arrive at a farmhouse in Maryland where Sarah has lived all of her life. It is the farmhouse her parents lived in while she was growing up. It is the house where she was first taught the scriptures of God's word, including the ten commandments. From a young age Sarah was taught by her farming parents as well as the church she grew up in. She applied the teaching of the ten commandments to her life and now in her old age she is living the promise of the fifth commandment: "Honor your father and your mother, so that you may live long in the land the Lord your God is giving you."

"Amnon you are looking at history here," said Benjamin.
"This farmhouse?" asked Amnon.
"Well, if you include Sarah, then yes," replied Benjamin. "But seriously, I am referring to Sarah and the long and illustrious life she has lived in her relationship .with God," said Benjamin. "You see Amnon, Sarah grew as a young girl living by the teaching of the ten commandments which encouraged her to come to saving

faith in Jesus Christ and living her life according to the teachings of all of God's word," Benjamin went on to say.

"Didn't Sarah grow up when the ten commandments were being eliminated in the public schools and public places?" asked Amnon.

"That's correct," replied Benjamin. "It was then that Sarah began to see the results of removing the ten commandments for all to see," said Benjamin. "As a young woman Sarah came to understand God's purpose in the creation of woman and how the removal of the ten commandments began to have a debilitating effect on young girls and women of all ages," continued Benjamin.

"What were the debilitating effects on women?" asked Amnon.

"Sarah, as well as many other Christian believers began to see young girls becoming promiscuous and indulging in immorality," replied Benjamin. "Women began having children without being married and sometimes having multiple children by multiple fathers," said Benjamin. "And then more women began having abortions as a result of their promiscuity and immoral lifestyles," continued Benjamin.

"Many women were experiencing divorce and remarriage issues, right, Benjamin?" asked Amnon.

"That's correct," replied Benjamin. "The crime of domestic violence between men and women began to rise as well as abuse of children in the home," said Benjamin.

"Girls and women just seemed to lose their self-identity, right, Benjamin?" asked Amnon.

"That's correct," replied Benjamin. "As Sarah was raising her own children in the teachings of God's word, it seemed as though girls and women did not know that they were created by God and for what purpose," said Benjamin. "Girls and women began living a lifestyle vastly different from how God had intended as spoken by the Apostle Paul in Romans 1:26, 'Because of this, God gave them over to shameful lusts. Even their women exchanged natural relations for unnatural ones,'" continued Benjamin.

"But the same thing was happening with boys and men, right, Benjamin?" asked Amnon.

"That's correct," replied Benjamin. "The Apostle Paul states in Romans 1:27-28 "In the same way the men also abandoned natural relations with women and were inflamed with lust for one another. Men committed indecent acts with other men and received in themselves the due penalty for their perversion," continued Benjamin.

"That's when the world began seeing a pandemic of the AIDS virus with the result of many deaths as well as legalized marriage between members of the same gender, right, Benjamin?" asked Amnon.

"That's correct," replied Benjamin. "But it hasn't stopped there," said Benjamin. "Sarah continued to minister God's word to young girls and women even after she became a grandmother because she was seeing the results of 2nd Corinthians 4:4, 'The god of this age has blinded the minds of unbelievers, so that they cannot see the light of the gospel of the glory of Christ, who is the image of God,'" said Benjamin.

"Benjamin, God's word says that such people will not enter the kingdom of God," said Amnon. "Listen to the words of the Apostle Paul in 1st Corinthians 6:9-10, 'Do you not know that the wicked will not inherit the kingdom of God? Do not be deceived: Neither the sexually immoral nor idolaters nor adulterers nor male prostitutes nor homosexual offenders nor thieves nor the greedy nor drunkards nor slanderers nor swindlers will inherit the kingdom of God,'" said Amnon quoting the Apostle Paul.

"And even as Sarah is at the end of her days as God has blessed her with old age yet the confusion of sexual identity in the lives of girls and boys and women and men continues to evolve into another realm," said Benjamin. "Boys and girls and men and women today struggle to identify with their gender identity as God created them," continued Benjamin.

"Listen to the words of the Apostle Paul in Romans 1:28, 'Furthermore, since they did not think it worthwhile to retain the knowledge of God, He gave them over to a depraved mind, to do what ought not to be done,'" said Amnon quoting the Apostle Paul.

"Benjamin, the Apostle Paul states in Romans 1:32 'Although they know God's righteous decree that those who do such things deserve death, they not only continue to do these very things but also approve of those who practice them,'" said Amnon.

"But even with all this confusion that results in sin Sarah shared the good news of 1st John 1:9, 'If we confess our sins, He is faithful and just and will forgive us our sins and purify us from all unrighteousness,'" said Benjamin.

CHAPTER TWENTY-ONE

      Benjamin and Amnon are ever close to Sarah as she lies in her bed with children and grandchildren visiting her. Sarah has experienced the joys and sorrows of life, the troubles and victories of life and the blessings of coming to know her Savior through the study of God's word as well as her prayer and worship life. Sarah has experienced spiritual warfare with her spiritual enemy like every other child of God. She has strived to live her Christian life so as to bring glory to her Lord and Savior, Jesus Christ.
      Sarah has experienced the aspects of growing older--the loss of physical strength and energy, the loss of physical endurance and beauty of youth, and even some slippage of memory from time to time. And though she has battled times of sickness, yet she experienced God's physical healing through His Son, Jesus, to continue on into old age. She experienced the blessings of a good marriage though her husband has already preceded her in death. She has experienced the blessings of having children that honor her as the fifth commandment commands to do. And she has been blessed with grandchildren who all know the Lord Jesus Christ as their Lord and Savior.

"Amnon, Sarah is a woman who reflects the words of King Solomon in Proverbs 31:10-12, 'A wife of noble character who can find? She is worth far more than rubies. Her husband has full confidence in her and lacks nothing of value. She brings him good, not harm, all the days of her life,' said Benjamin quoting the words of King Solomon.

"Benjamin, King Solomon goes on to say in Proverbs 31:25-31, 'She is clothed with strength and dignity; she can laugh at the days to come. She speaks with wisdom, and faithful instruction is on her tongue. She watches over the affairs of her household and does not eat the bread of idleness. Her children arise and call her blessed; her husband also, and he praises her: Many women do noble things, but you surpass them all. Charm is deceptive and beauty is fleeting; but a woman who fears the Lord is to be praised. Give her the reward she has earned, and let her works bring her praise at the city gate,'" said Amnon quoting King Solomon.

"Amnon, in light of the life Sarah has lived and the ministry she has conducted, make no mistake, God blessed her with a long life," said Benjamin. "The Psalmist promises in Psalm 91:14-16, 'Because he loves me, says the Lord, I will rescue him; I will protect him for he acknowledges my name. He will call upon me, and I will answer him; I will be with him in trouble, I will deliver him and honor him. With long life I will satisfy him and show him my salvation,'" said Benjamin quoting the Psalmist.

"Revelation 14:13 'Then I heard a voice from heaven say, 'Write: Blessed are the dead who die in the Lord from now on.' Yes, says the Spirit, 'they will rest from their labor, for their deeds will follow them,'" said Amnon.

Servants of the Most High God

Right then, Sarah, in her old age died of natural causes, leaving this temporal life, and going through death's door into eternity. But like all Christian believers when they die Benjamin and Amnon were there to catch her spirit into their hands so as to carry her spirit to heaven. Her time of labor is over, and her time of rest has come.

"Hello, Sarah, I am Benjamin, and this is Amnon, we are two of God's holy angels who are going to carry your spirit to heaven," said Benjamin.

"It seems as though I've been waiting forever for this day to come," replied Sarah.

"It seems that God blessed you with the longevity of days in this earthly life," replied Amnon. "But in reality, the long number of years God blessed you with cannot compare to eternity," continued Amnon.

"But in my old age not only was I believing in heaven, but I was actually looking forward to heaven," replied Sarah. "I'm looking forward to seeing my Savior face to face," continued Sarah.

"Well, just relax and we'll have you there in just a moment," said Amnon.

One moment later Sarah was standing at the ever-open door to heaven. As she walked into heaven, she found herself in a state of awe. Heaven was greater than she ever imagined. The glory of God and His Son shone brightly as she heard the great multitudes of angels and Christian brethren in worship to God. There before her was the One she was longing to see--Jesus.

Rick Stem

With arms open wide Jesus embraced her with a heavenly hug and said, welcome home, Sarah, I have been praying for you a long time. Please enter into worship with all who are here," Jesus continued.

Benjamin and Amnon entered into worship as well before they left for their next assignment. In the service they do, their assignments are always interesting and individualistically new. And yet God knows each one and His Son, Jesus, died for each one. They are all God's children. And Benjamin and Amnon delight in bringing God's children home.

CHAPTER TWENTY-TWO

Tribulation Saints

Benjamin took some time to discuss a yet future time when he and Amnon and all the other angels who carry the spirits of deceased Christian believers to heaven when they die as being a time when they will be extremely busy. It will be a time of great distress in the world--a time befittingly called the Great Tribulation Period--a period that will last seven years.

"Amnon, there's a time coming when we will be extremely busy," said Benjamin. "It'll be a time when multitudes of Christian believers around the world will lose their lives to Satan because of their faith in Jesus Christ," continued Benjamin. "In fact, listen to the words spoken by the Apostle John in Revelation 7:9, 'After this I looked and there before me was a great multitude that no one could count, from every nation, tribe, people, and language, standing before the throne and in front of the Lamb. They were wearing white robes and were holding palm branches in their hands. And they cried out in a loud voice: 'Salvation belongs to our God, who sits on the throne, and to the Lamb,'" continued Benjamin quoting the Apostle John.

"Are these the ones we will be busy taking to heaven?" asked Amnon.

"They are," replied Benjamin. "Listen to the words of the Apostle John in Revelation 7:13-14, 'Then one of the elders asked me, 'These in white robes--who are they, and where did they come from?' I answered, 'Sir, you know.' And he said, 'These are they who have come out of the great tribulation; they have washed their robes and made them white in the blood of the Lamb,'" replied Benjamin as he quoted the Apostle John.

"A large number of God's children will be going home," said Amnon. "These will be those who will not bow the knee to Satan, nor take the mark of the beast, because of their faith in Jesus," continued Amnon.

"But first, there will be another event that will actually rescue God's children from ever experiencing even the timing of this period of tribulation," replied Benjamin.

"I know, it's called the rapture of the church," said Amnon. "In fact, Jesus first told His disciples of this coming event as stated by the Apostle John in John 14:1-3, 'Do not let your hearts be troubled. Trust in God; trust also in me. In my Father's house are many rooms; if it were not so, I would have told you. I am going there to prepare a place for you. And if I go and prepare a place for you, I will come back and take you to be with me so that you also may be with me where I am,'" continued Amnon quoting the Apostle John.

"Jesus told the Apostle John speaking to the church of Philadelphia that Christian believers, also referred to as the Church, are exempt from this period of tribulation," said Benjamin. "Listen to Jesus' words to the Church of

Philadelphia in Revelation 3:10, 'Since you have kept my command to endure patiently, I will also keep you from the hour of trial that is going to come upon the whole world to test those who live on the earth,'" continued Benjamin quoting Jesus.

"That's because God has not appointed the Church for wrath, right Benjamin?" asked Amnon.

"That's correct," replied Benjamin. "Listen to the Apostle Paul's words in 1st Thessalonians 5:9, 'For God did not appoint us to suffer wrath but to receive salvation through our Lord Jesus Christ,'" said Benjamin quoting the Apostle Paul.

"And though Jesus promised of this event to come He never said when it would happen, right, Benjamin?" asked Amnon.

"That's correct," replied Benjamin. "But it is an imminent event which means that it can happen any day, and there are no signs pointing to its timing," continued Benjamin.

"So Christian believers should always be alert and watchful, right, Benjamin?" asked Amnon.

"That's correct," replied Benjamin. "Listen to the Apostle Paul's words as he encouraged the Thessalonian believers in 1st Thessalonians 5:4-6, 'But you, brothers, are not in darkness so that this day should surprise you like a thief. You are all sons of the light and sons of the day. We do not belong to the night or to the darkness. So then, let us not be like others, who are asleep, but let us be alert and self-controlled,'" continued Benjamin quoting the Apostle Paul.

"And didn't the Apostle Peter warn Christian believers about losing faith while waiting for the rapture?" asked Amnon.

"He sure did," replied Benjamin. "Listen to the Apostle Peter's words in 2nd Peter 3:3-4, 'First of all, you must understand that in the last days scoffers will come, scoffing and following their own evil desires. They will say, 'Where is this coming, he promised? Ever since our fathers died, everything goes on as it has since the beginning of creation,'" continued Benjamin quoting the Apostle Peter.

"But it's surely going to happen, right, Benjamin?" asked Amnon.

"Most definitely," replied Benjamin. "But it's an event only for Christian believers," said Benjamin as he quoted the words of the Apostle Paul in 1st Thessalonians 4:13-17, "Brothers, we do not want you to be ignorant about those who fall asleep, or to grieve like the rest of men, who have no hope. We believe that Jesus died and rose again and so we believe that God will bring with Jesus those who have fallen asleep in Him. According to the Lord's own word, we tell you that we who are still alive, who are left till the coming of the Lord, will certainly not precede those who have fallen asleep. For the Lord Himself will come down from heaven, with a loud command, with the voice of the archangel and with the trumpet call of God, and the dead in Christ will rise first. After that, we who are still alive and are left will be caught up together with them in the clouds to meet the Lord in the air. And so we will be with the Lord forever."

Servants of the Most High God

CHAPTER TWENTY-THREE

Benjamin continued to discuss the rapture of the church and the nature of this glorious event. Benjamin reminded Amnon that those who have not yet put saving faith in Jesus Christ as their Lord and Savior will not experience the rapture of the church nor even witness it taking place.

"Non-Christians will not participate in the rapture nor see it happen, right, Benjamin?" asked Amnon.

"That's correct," replied Benjamin. "Listen to the words of the Apostle Paul as he explains the nature of the rapture in 1st Corinthians 15:50-53, 'I declare to you, brothers, that flesh and blood cannot inherit the kingdom of God, nor does the perishable inherit the imperishable. Listen, I tell you a mystery: We will not all sleep, but we will all be changed--in a flash, in the twinkling of an eye, at the last trumpet. For the trumpet will sound, the dead will be raised imperishable, and we will be changed,'" continued Benjamin as he quoted the Apostle Paul.

"Will this affect the spirits of the deceased Christian believers that we angels have carried to heaven?" asked Amnon.

"Absolutely!" exclaimed Benjamin. "According to 1st Thessalonians 4:13-17, when the rapture of the Church occurs, the spirits of the deceased Christian believers that we angels have carried to heaven will return with Jesus from heaven to the clouds in the air and at Jesus' shout and command those spirits' bodies will be resurrected and gloriously changed into the same glorified body that Jesus has--a body that will not suffer sickness, death, deformities, decay or weaknesses in any way, including old age," continued Benjamin. "Listen to the words of Luke as he describes a conversation that the resurrected Jesus had with His disciples in Luke 24:38-43, 'He said to them, 'Why are you troubled, and why do doubts rise in your minds? Look at my hands and my feet. It is I, myself! Touch me and see; a ghost does not have flesh and bones, as you see I have.' When He said this, He showed them His hands and feet. And while they still did not believe it because of joy and amazement, He asked them, 'Do you have anything here to eat?' They gave Him a piece of broiled fish, and He took it and ate it in their presence,'" continued Benjamin quoting the words of Luke.

"And those Christian believers who are still alive when the rapture of the Church takes place will not die but will be raised up to the clouds and in that instantaneous process their bodies will be changed into the same glorious body that Jesus has, right, Benjamin?" asked Amnon.

"You got it Amnon," replied Benjamin.
"Jesus will then take them to heaven to the Father's house as He calls it in John 14:2, right, Benjamin?" asked Amnon.

"That's correct," replied Benjamin. "And after the rapture occurs all Christian believers will stand before Jesus at the Judgement seat of Christ to give an account of how each Christian believer lived his or her life for Jesus," continued Benjamin.

Servants of the Most High God

"Is that when Christian believers in heaven will receive rewards and crowns?" asked Amnon.

"That's correct Amnon," replied Benjamin. "Listen to the Apostle Paul's words in 2nd Corinthians 5:10, 'For we must all appear before the judgement seat of Christ, that each one may receive what is due him for the things done while in the body, whether good or bad,'" continued Benjamin as he quoted the Apostle Paul.

"By chance, Benjamin, is that who the Apostle John saw when Jesus invited him to heaven?" asked Amnon.

"No doubt about it Amnon, the twenty-four elders John saw represent the raptured church saints in heaven before the Great Tribulation Period begins," replied Benjamin. "Listen to the Apostle John's words in Revelation 4:4, 'Surrounding the throne were twenty-four other thrones, and seated on them were twenty-four elders,' and who according to Revelation 4:10-11, 'the twenty-four elders fall down before Him who sits on the throne, and worship Him who lives forever and ever. They lay their crowns before the throne and say: 'You are worthy, our Lord and God, to receive glory and honor and power, for you created all things, and by your will they were created and have their being,'" continued Benjamin as he quoted the Apostle John.

"But when does the time come when we angels are to be extremely busy carrying the spirits of deceased Christian believers to heaven?" asked Amnon. "It sounds like we will have a temporary break in our service to God once the Church is called up out of the world and taken to heaven," continued Amnon.

"First, do you understand thus far the details and elements of the resurrection and rapture event?" asked Benjamin.

"Got it!" exclaimed Amnon.

Rick Stem

"Okay, let me explain the time where we will be very busy," said Benjamin.

CHAPTER TWENTY-FOUR

Benjamin now turned his teaching to the time right after the rapture of the church and the activities that will lead to that time when he and Amnon and all the other angels who serve the Most High God in taking God's children home will be most busy.

"As soon as the rapture of the church takes place there will be no Christian believers left in the world--they will have all been raptured," said Benjamin.

"So that means only non-believers--those who do not believe in Jesus Christ and those who have rejected His great salvation will have been left behind so to speak?" asked Amnon.

"Right on, Amnon," replied Benjamin. "And let me describe the people that will be left after the rapture takes place as given by the Apostle Paul's description of the works of the flesh as he describes in Galatians 5:19-21, 'The acts of the sinful nature are obvious: sexual immorality, impurity, and debauchery; idolatry and witchcraft; hatred, discord, jealousy, fits of rage, selfish ambition, factions and envy, drunkenness, orgies, and the like. I warn you, as I did before, that those who live like this will not inherit the kingdom of God," continued Benjamin as he quoted the Apostle Paul.

"So, it's possible that some who professed to be a Christian believer may miss the rapture and be left behind because they weren't true Christian believers, is that possible, Benjamin?" asked Amnon.

"Quite possible," replied Benjamin. "Listen to the words of Jesus as He addressed the church of Laodicea in Revelation 3:14-17, 'To the angel of the church in Laodicea write: These are the words of the Amen, the faithful and true witness, the ruler of God's creation. I know your deeds, that you are neither cold nor hot. I wish you were either one or the other! So, because you are lukewarm--neither hot nor cold--I am about to spit you out of my mouth. You say, I am rich; I have acquired wealth and do not need a thing. But you do not realize that you are wretched, pitiful, poor, blind, and naked,'" continued Benjamin quoting the words of Jesus.

"But even that being the case, those who are living like the Laodiceans today can still make a change before it's too late, can't they?" asked Amnon.

"They surely can," replied Benjamin. "Listen to Jesus' further words to the Laodiceans in Revelation 3:19-22, 'Those whom I love I rebuke and discipline. So be earnest, and repent. Here I am! I stand at the door and knock. If anyone hears my voice and opens the door, I will come in and eat with him, and he with me. To him who overcomes I will give the right to sit with me on my throne, just as I overcame and sat down with my Father on His throne. He who has an ear, let him hear what the Spirit says to the churches,'" continued Benjamin quoting Jesus.

"Man, who wouldn't want to participate in the rapture of the Church?" asked Amnon. "Meeting Jesus in the clouds and for the first time living Christian believers will actually see Him who for now they live unto by faith!"

exclaimed Amnon. "On top of that they will be reunited with loved ones who had died and their spirits were carried to heaven by us angels and they will be in their new glorified bodies at that," continued Amnon. "Christian believers living at the time of the rapture will experience the glory of heaven that we angels have always known since our creation!" exclaimed Amnon.

"Sad to say, though, Amnon, that for those who miss the rapture and are left behind they are going to experience tribulation and distress that they cannot imagine," said Benjamin.

"But God has declared in His word consisting of the holy scriptures contained in the Holy Bible what exactly is going to occur and when, right, Benjamin?" asked Amnon.

"God has always known what is to occur and when it will occur and because He desires none to perish, He has declared it all in His word--nothing is left out or hidden," replied Benjamin. "Satan will be given freedom to commit all the evil he wants to do because God will sovereignly use him and the evil he does to judge this unbelieving and rejecting world," continued Benjamin.

"But God will also pour forth His wrath of judgement through the realms of His physical creation as well, right, Benjamin?" asked Amnon.

"Your ever so right," replied Benjamin. "In fact, Jesus told His disciples just how bad things will get in that seven-year period known as the Great Tribulation Period as stated in Matthew 24:21, 'For then there will be great distress, unequaled from the beginning of the world until now--and never to be equaled again,'" continued Benjamin quoting the words of Jesus.

"This is when things will bring about the time when we angels will be extremely busy, right, Benjamin?" asked Amnon.

"That's right Amnon," let me explain it to you," replied Benjamin.

CHAPTER TWENTY-FIVE

Benjamin began to explain the upcoming events that will come upon the whole world now that the rapture of the Church has taken place. God is going to bring His judgement upon the entire world because the world turned down His offer of love, mercy, and grace which was demonstrated through the salvation provided through His Son, Jesus Christ. Believe it or not, God will actually use Satan to bring about some of His judgement. And even though God will bring about judgement on the entire world, yet He will also demonstrate His love for sinful man in that He will raise up preachers to proclaim the gospel message of salvation to those who will believe it and receive it.

"After the rapture of the Church the world will be in a state of great chaos and distress," said Benjamin. "Satan will bring his man--the Antichrist, on the scene to bring about order to the chaos in the world as well as bring a temporary and false peace to the evil and violence in the world before he does his evil work," continued Benjamin.

"The Antichrist's nature will be just like Satan's nature which will bring evil situations about as Satan works at controlling the affairs of men throughout the whole world," said Benjamin. "In fact, the Great Tribulation Period will start when the Antichrist enters a peace proposal with God's chosen people--the nation of Israel," continued Benjamin.

"How bad will things get under the Antichrist?" asked Amnon. "Will there be any hope for anyone?" asked Amnon.

"The Antichrist will eventually lead a one world government with a one world economy supported by a one world religion," replied Benjamin. "Eventually the Antichrist will replace the one world religion by requiring all people to worship him," said Benjamin. "Listen to the Apostle John's words in Revelation 13:8, 'All inhabitants of the earth will worship the beast--all whose names have not been written in the book of life belonging to the Lamb that was slain from the creation of the world,' " continued Benjamin.

"How will anyone get their names written in the Lamb's book of life?" asked Amnon.

"During the time of chaos and distress followed by God bringing forth His judgements on the world, some of which He will be using Satan and his man, the Antichrist, God will raise up 144,000 Jewish evangelists to preach the gospel message of salvation," said Benjamin. "God will seal them and protect them from any harm from Satan's man, the Antichrist," continued Benjamin. "Listen to the words of the Apostle John as he describes their ministry in Revelation 7:2-3, 'Then I saw another angel coming up from the east, having the seal of the living God. He called out in a loud voice to the four angels who had been given power to harm the land and the sea: 'Do not harm the land or the sea or the trees until we have put a seal on the foreheads of the servants of our God,' Then I heard the number of those who were sealed: 144,000 from all the tribes of Israel,' " said Benjamin as he quoted the Apostle

John. "Besides these 144,00 Jewish evangelists preaching the gospel message of salvation God will have two witnesses in Jerusalem doing likewise as well as one of His angels flying around the world proclaiming the gospel message of salvation to everyone," continued Benjamin.

"So, during the beginning of this period of great tribulation God will have all these Jewish evangelists, two witnesses in Jerusalem, and an angel flying worldwide preaching a worldwide revival while Satan is working through his man, the Antichrist, to kill everyone who becomes a believer in Jesus Christ and does not worship him?" asked Amnon.

"You got it," replied Benjamin. "Listen to the words of the Apostle John in Revelation 6:9-11, 'When he opened the fifth seal, I saw under the altar the souls of those who had been slain because of the word of God and the testimony they had maintained. They called out in a loud voice, 'How long, Sovereign Lord, holy and true, until you judge the inhabitants of the earth and avenge our blood?' Then each of them was given a white robe, and they were told to wait a little longer, until the number of their fellow servants and brothers who were to be killed as they had been was completed,'" continued Benjamin as he quoted the words of the Apostle John.

"So, this is that period of time to come when you and I and the other angels will be very busy?" asked Amnon.

"That's the time that will be coming," replied Benjamin. "As I have already stated from Revelation chapter seven, it will be a great multitude no one can count from every nation, tribe, people, and language," continued Benjamin.

"So, God will demonstrate His desire for none to perish as the Apostle Peter says in 2nd Peter 3:8-9, 'But do not forget this one thing dear friends: With the Lord a day is like a thousand years, and a thousand years are like a day. The Lord is not slow in keeping His promise as some understand slowness. He is patient with you, not wanting anyone to perish, but everyone to come to repentance,'" said Amnon.

"Amnon, EVERYONE WILL DIE, except for that one special group of people that will be alive when the rapture of the Church occurs," said Benjamin. "Listen to what the author of Hebrews states in reference to death, judgement, and salvation in Hebrews 9:27-28, 'Just as man is destined to die once, and after that to face judgement, so Christ was sacrificed once to take away the sins of many people; and He will appear a second time, not to bear sin, but to bring salvation to those who are waiting for Him,' " continued Benjamin as he quoted the author of Hebrews.

"Benjamin, as we are very aware, everyday many thousands of people wake up not knowing it is their last day of life--they will unexpectedly enter through death's door into eternity," said Amnon. "Listen to the words of the Apostle Paul in 2nd Corinthians 6:1-3, 'As God's fellow workers we urge you not to receive God's grace in vain. For he says, 'In the time of my favor I heard you, and on the day of salvation I helped you.' I tell you, now is the time of God's favor; now is the day of salvation,'" continued Amnon as he quoted the words of the Apostle Paul.

As Benjamin and Amnon are in route to their next assignment they reflect on that future time to come when they will be most busy, but they are also reminded how busy they are now. They reflect on the great joy they have in their service to God in carrying the spirits of Christian believers to heaven when they die. They serve their creator God in all faithfulness and obedience as they fulfill God's

Servants of the Most High God
decree to them, SERVANTS OF THE MOST HIGH GOD, BRING MY CHILDREN HOME!

Rick Stem

www.ingramcontent.com/pod-product-compliance
Lightning Source LLC
Chambersburg PA
CBHW071459070526
44578CB00001B/396